Brewing Quality Beers:

The Home Brewer's Essential Guidebook

by

Byron Burch

*Paddy,
Best wishes always to a fine brewer!*

Joby Books
P.O. Box 512
Fulton, CA 95439

DEDICATION

To Alicia Laurel, Sierra Joy,
Neva Vineyard, and Robyn Sequoia

ACKNOWLEDGMENTS

So much time has passed that it's no longer possible to even remember all the people I've traded ideas with over the past fifteen years, but each conversation, each phone call for advice, and each joint sampling of our mutual efforts, has made a contribution to this book. I must, however, mention two persons I've worked with for several years, Nancy Vineyard and Jay Conner. We've learned and taught together. Nancy, along with Jay Reed, also did the book's photography.

One noteworthy development which followed the legalization of home brewing in 1979 was the opening of communication between home brewers and many commercial brewers. I would especially like to thank Brian Hunt from Xcelsior Brewing Co. of Santa Rosa, California; Gary Bauer from Vienna Brewing Co. of Milwaukee, Wisconsin; and Fritz Maytag from Anchor Brewing Co. of San Francisco, California; each of whom has been particularly helpful to me in one way or another.

INTRODUCTION

A dozen years ago I began my first book on home brewing by pointing out that the hobby had gone through a vast number of changes since the strange tasting, bottle exploding days of prohibition. It was true. Technology and ingredients had made vast improvements and home brewing had moved out of the dark ages. However, those of us who were brewing back then really thought we'd gone about as far as home brewers would ever go. With a surpassing naivete, we saw ourselves participating in the high renaissance of home brewing. Little did we know it was only the late middle ages that had been reached.

With formal legalization, which came in 1979, everything changed. The U.S. Government was no longer telling commercial brewery people not to talk to home brewers and suddenly we began to find many brewers willing to exchange information with us. Many suppliers to the brewing industry also began to sell to home brew supply shops. Suddenly, the kinds of hops and malt grains available to home brewers was several times what it had been.

In short, though we'd been making very good beers for a number of years, there were now better and more varied ways to do so. With so many possible combinations, the creative challenge was unprecedented, and home brewing emerged as an endlessly fascinating hobby.

After such a spurt of growth, it was apparent *Quality Brewing,* despite its best seller status, needed revising and updating, so a year ago the task began. As the work went on, however, I began to find fewer and fewer passages escaping unchanged. Obviously, what was taking shape was really a new book. There are a few things from the old one which have been carried on for the sake of continuity, some drawings and photographs and a handful of paragraphs I was unable to improve, but this is a minute percentage of the whole.

As before, my purpose is to educate home brewers, helping them to make excellent beers. You'll be guided through the mixing and boiling of the initial "wort" (your brew before it ferments), and on into the "magical," living, fermentation process which transforms it into finished beer.

If you're a beginner, read through the book, and then make up a batch from the selection of ale and stout recipes. After you've done one, read the book again. Much information will come into focus once you've actually gone through the process. Note that a number of unfamiliar terms will be introduced shortly, but don't worry about them. They'll be explained later.

Note also that this book gives all temperatures in Fahrenheit, with the Celsius reading in parentheses. If a temperature range is given for fermentation, best results will be obtained by striving for the lower end of the range. This shouldn't discourage someone lacking the facilities for temperature control, but be aware that beers can be improved by such control.

Canadian and British readers should be aware that U.S. measurements are being used. A table of equivalents appears on page 66. Metric equivalents are given in parentheses throughout the text whenever exact measurement is required. However, such common measurements as teaspoons, tablespoons, and cups are likely to be part of our households for quite some time, and have been retained.

In the U.S., legalization means that in most states a single person is allowed to make up to 100 gallons each of beer and wine per year, while the head of a household is allowed 200 gallons of each. Obviously, this formal recognition was very important to the home brew movement, which has grown dramatically in the years since. Most major cities, and a number of smaller ones, now have supply shops for home brewers and winemakers. Check the yellow pages under "Wine Makers' Equipment and Supplies," and "Beer Homebrewing Equipment and Supplies." A number of these firms are equipped to handle mail order service, which will be helpful if you live some distance away.

It's time to go on and look at the brewing process. We start with the procedure for ales and stouts because these beers are delightful, easy to make, and ready relatively soon. We'll look at lagers later on.

PROCEDURE FOR ALES AND STOUTS

Cooking

If you will be using any grain malts except the black grains, start at point "A." If you are not, start at point "B."

A. If your recipe contains Lager, Pale, Mild Ale, Munich, Crystal, or Wheat Malt, place the cracked or ground grain in a kitchen pan, cover with water, heat to approximately 150 degrees F (66 C.), cover and let stand (either on the stove top or in the oven) for 45 minutes to an hour before you're actually ready to start to work.

Place a colander over your boiling kettle and pour in the grain, letting the water collect in the pot below. Rinse through the grain with hot water, at least 130 degrees F. (54 C.) but no hotter than 170 F. (77 C.), until a clear runoff is obtained. Discard the grain. The liquid becomes part of the boil.

B. If your recipe doesn't call for these malts, omit the above steps, and go directly to the boiling of the wort as follows.

Thoroughly dissolve any of the following called for in your recipe: Malt Extract, Dry Malt, any Sugar except priming sugar, Rice Syrup, Dextrin Powder, Gypsum, Salt, Epsom Salts, Irish Moss, or Yeast Nutrient, in two or more gallons of water (as much as possible). Heat to a rolling boil. Stir in half of the Bittering Hops and boil for 30 minutes, stirring occasionally. Add the rest of the Bittering Hops (along with any Roasted Barley, Black Patent Malt, or Chocolate Malt called for) and boil for 30 more minutes, adding the Aromatic Hops during the last two minutes.*

At the end of the boil, the wort should be cooled as quickly as possible to a temperature between 70 and 85 degrees F. (21–27 C.), so the yeast can be added.

* If you are using hop pellets, you may "dry hop" by adding your aromatic hops to the fermentor just prior to fermentation instead of putting them in the boiling kettle.

Fermentation

Siphon your cooled wort into one or more sanitized glass jugs, filling them no more than two thirds full. Add the yeast, attach a fermentation lock to each container, and allow the fermentation to procede. In five to seven days, when apparent yeast activity has ceased, the saccharometer reading is somewhere near where it's supposed to be, and the sample you're testing tastes like dry, flat beer, it's time to get ready for bottling.

Bottling

When fermentation is complete, ales and stouts are ready for bottling. If you have not already added all the water to your brew, pour it into a sanitized plastic bucket (or your boiling kettle if it's 6½ gallons or larger). Siphon your beer into the same container, taking care to avoid splashing it. Boil up your Priming Sugar Syrup and stir it in thoroughly. Siphon the primed beer into your bottles and cap them. Check your ales after a week or so. If carbonated, they may be enjoyed immediately, though some will improve with a bit more time in the bottle. Sit back, then, and enjoy the fruits of your labors. This is what it's all about. The best time to enjoy one of your beers, by the way, is while cooking up a new batch.

Ale and Stout Recipes

1. Light Ale—5 U.S. gal. (19 liters)

3½ lbs. (1.6 kilos) Light Malt Extract
2 tsp. Gypsum
1½ lbs. (681 grams) Corn Sugar
⅛ tsp. Salt
2 oz. (57 grams) Bittering Hops (Northern Brewer or Bullion)
½ oz. (14 grams) Aromatic Hops (Fuggle or Cascade)
Water to 5 gallons (19 liters)
¾ cup Corn Sugar for priming
1 tsp. Yeast Nutrient
½ oz. (14 grams) Ale Yeast

Starting S.G.   1.036
Final S.G.   1.006–8
Alcohol by vol. 3½%

2. Pale Ale—5 U.S. gal. (19 liters)

5 lbs. (2.3 kilos) Light Dry Malt or 6 lbs. (2.7 kilos) Light Malt
   Extract
1 lb. (454 grams) Crystal Malt
1–2 tsp. Gypsum
½ tsp. Salt
1½ oz. (43 grams) Bittering Hops (Nugget or Eroica)
½ oz. Aromatic Hops (Fuggle or Cascade)
Water to 5 gallons (19 liters)
¾ cup Corn Sugar for priming
½ oz. (14 grams) Ale Yeast

Starting S.G.   1.044–1.048
Final S.G.   1.011–1.012
Alcohol by vol. 4%

3. British Style Bitter—5 U.S. gal. (19 liters)

6½ lbs. (3 kilos) Amber Malt Extract
1 lb. (454 grams) Crystal Malt
2 oz. (57 grams) 100% Dextrin Powder (optional)
1–2 tsp. Gypsum
½ tsp. Salt
2 oz. (57 grams) Bittering Hops (Northern Brewer or Bullion) or 1½
   oz. (42 grams) Bittering Hops (Nugget or Eroica)
½ oz. (14 grams) Aromatic Hops (Fuggle, Willamette, Cascade or
   East Kent Golding)
Water to 5 gallons (19 liters)
¾ cup Corn Sugar for priming
½ oz. (14 grams) Ale Yeast

Starting S.G.   1.050
Final S.G.   1.012–15
Alcohol by vol. 5%

4. Scottish Style Brown Ale—5 U.S. gal. (19 liters)

4½ lbs. (2.1 kilos) Light Dry Malt
8 oz. (227 grams) Crystal Malt
2 oz. (57 grams) Munich Malt
3½ oz. (99 grams) Crushed Chocolate Malt (added to mash)
8 oz. (227 grams) Dark Brown Sugar
4 oz. (113 grams) 100% Dextrin Powder
½ tsp. Gypsum
¾ tsp. Salt
2 oz. (57 grams) Bittering Hops (Fuggle or Willamette)
1 oz. (28 grams) Aromatic Hops (Northern Brewer dry hopped)
Water to 5 gallons (19 liters)
¾ cup Corn Sugar for priming
½ oz. (14 grams) Ale Yeast

Starting S.G.   1.047
Final S.G.   1.015
Alcohol by vol. 5%

5. Porter—5 U.S. gal. (19 liters)

5 lbs. (2.3 kilos) Light Dry Malt or 6 lbs. (2.7 kilos) Light Malt
   Extract
2 lbs. (907 grams) Crystal Malt
1½ lbs. (681 grams) Munich Malt
4 oz. (113 grams) Chocolate Malt (added to boil)
4 oz. (113 grams) Black Patent Malt (added to boil)
4 to 6 oz. (113 to 170 grams) 100% Dextrin Powder (optional)
¼ tsp. Salt
1¾ oz. (50 grams) Bittering Hops (Nugget or Eroica)
1 oz. (28 grams) Aromatic Hops (Fuggle, Willamette or Cascade)
Water to 5 gallons (19 liters)
¾ cup Corn Sugar for priming
½ oz. (14 grams) Ale Yeast

Starting S.G.   1.050
Final S.G.   1.015
Alcohol by vol. 5%

6. Irish Style Stout—5 U.S. gal. (19 liters)

5 lbs. (2.3 kilos) Light Dry Malt or 6 lbs. (2.7 kilos) Light Malt
   Extract
2 lbs. (907 grams) Amber or Dark Malt Extract
1 lb. (454 grams) Roasted Barley (added to boil)
¼ tsp. Salt
2½ oz. (71 grams) Bittering Hops (Northern Brewer or Bullion)
½ oz. (14 grams) Aromatic Hops (Fuggle, Willamette, Cascade or
   Styrian Golding)
Water to 5 gallons (19 liters)
¾ cup Corn Sugar for priming
½ oz. (14 grams) Ale Yeast

Starting S.G.   1.058
Final S.G.   1.020
Alcohol by vol. 5%

7. Imperial Stout*—5 U.S. gal. (19 liters)

8 lbs. (3.6 kilos) Dark Dry Malt
1 lb. (454 grams) Crystal Malt
8 oz. (227 grams) Black Patent Malt (Crushed and Boiled)
5 lbs. (2.3 kilos) White Rice Syrup
1 lb. (454 grams) Corn Sugar
¼ tsp. Salt
Bittering Hops: 3 oz. (85 grams) Northern Brewer or Bullion and 2
   oz. (57 grams) Nugget or Eroica
Aromatic Hops: 2 oz. (57 grams) Cascade and ¼ oz. (7 grams)
   Saaz (dry hopped)
Water to 5 Gallons (19 liters)
¾ cup Corn Sugar for priming
½ oz. (14 grams) Pasteur Champagne Wine Yeast

Starting S.G.   1.095
Final S.G.   1.035
Alcohol by vol. 7%

* Note that this beer will require several months in the bottle to
mature. It will introduce you to a special class of strong beers
known as "Barley Wines." Here's another.

8. Barley Wine—5 U.S. gal. (19 liters)

8 lbs. (3.6 kilos) Light Dry Malt
3 lbs. (1.4 kilos) Crystal Malt
1½ lbs. (681 grams) Mild Ale or Munich Malt
1½ oz. (43 grams) Chocolate Malt (added to mash)
8 oz. (227 grams) 100% Dextrin Powder
Bittering Hops: 2 oz. (28 grams) Eroica
Aromatic Hops: 3 oz. (85 grams) Cascade (dry hopped)
Water to 5 gallons (19 liters)
¾ cup Corn Sugar for priming
½ oz. (14 grams) Pasteur Champagne Wine Yeast

Starting S.G.   1.105
Final S.G.   1.030
Alcohol by vol. 8%

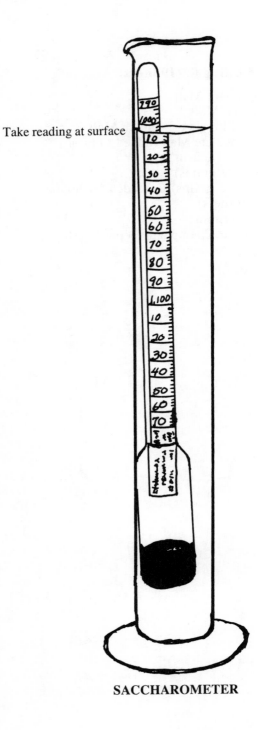

Take reading at surface

SACCHAROMETER

NECESSARY EQUIPMENT

If you're a beginner reading this for the first time, you're probably bewildered by now by the mass of unfamiliar terms swarming about your head. Don't panic, though, because explanations are coming up starting here. It should also be said, for the sake of reassurance, that once you have brewed one or two batches, the basic process will be rather routine. Thus encouraged, hopefully you're ready for some detailed discussion and advice concerning equipment, ingredients, and those procedures which aren't self-explanatory. We start with the equipment.

1. A Boiling Kettle. This should be a stainless steel or enamel kettle of at least four gallon capacity. If possible, get one that is at least eight or ten gallons so you can boil the entire wort at once. This will help with sanitation. If not, you'll have to boil some water with the malt and hops making up the difference with water that has been boiled previously. I personally recommend stainless steel as a better investment in the long run, because it won't chip like enamel canners will, exposing bare metal. Obviously, stainless steel is expensive, so here, as elsewhere, the home brewer must establish his own trade-off between ease, expense and quality.

2. A Saccharometer. This is a hydrometer designed to measure by weight the amount of sugar in a given solution. A small amount of beer or wort is drawn off into a testing jar (graduated cylinder). The saccharometer, an elongated, hollow glass instrument weighted at the bottom and calibrated along the stem-like upper part, is placed in the liquid, spun around to dislodge air bubbles, and allowed to float freely. When it stabilizes, a reading is taken right at the surface of the liquid, at the bottom of the "meniscus," the slight clinging of the solution to the sides of the saccharometer and test jar.

Since sugar is heavier than water, though alcohol is lighter, a saccharometer, which has a constant weight, will float higher in a sugar solution (such as unfermented wort) than in plain water or an alcohol solution. The more sugar there is, the higher it floats.

The saccharometer has two functions in home brewing. First the fermentation process is yeast acting on sugar, converting it into alcohol, as well as carbon dioxide (which escapes as a gas). Therefore, measuring the amount of sugars present in the initial wort allows you to calculate in advance the potential strength of your brew. Second, arriving at or near the expected final reading and stopping, it tells you when fermentation is complete more reliably than does the mere absence of apparent activity. In short, it allows you to be more exact about what you are doing.

Saccharometers can be calibrated according to the Balling (Brix) scale or the Specific Gravity scale. Though Balling is used in the wine and beer industries, Specific Gravity is a more exact scale and it is used here for that reason. Many saccharometers come calibrated with both, along wih a potential alcohol scale which can be useful as well.

On the Specific Gravity scale 1.000 is the weight of water, with higher numbers indicating additional weight, such as in sugar solutions. Because the range brewers are concerned with primarily involves the two right hand places, it is customary to refer to these digits only to simplify communication. Thus S.G. 1.000 is called "zero," S.G. 1.035 is "35," S.G. 1.045 is "45," and so on. This book follows the practice from here on.

If your saccharometer only gives the Balling scale, use the table on page 64 to make the conversion.

Note, of course, that if you are taking a reading before all the water has been added to a five gallon batch, you will need to adjust your readings. Thus, a specific gravity of 50 with four gallons of water added would be 40 when the fifth gallon was included. To get the actual reading in this situation, multiply the reading by the number of gallons actually present and divide the result by the total number of gallons it will eventually have. This adjustment is also necessary for final gravities.

Note also that beer used for a test sample should not be returned to the batch, so chances of contamination are minimized.

3. A Thermometer. An immersible, wide-range, dairy type thermometer with a range of roughly 20–200 degrees F. (–7 to 94 C.) is excellent. If, however, you're quite sure you will eventually go on to advanced (all-grain) brewing, you may wish to invest in a 10 to 12 inch, metal, probe thermometer which will give you an almost instantaneous reading.

4. Fermenting and Bottling Containers. When your wort has been boiled and cooled, it has to be fermented. Siphon it into one or more sanitized glass jugs, filling them no more than two thirds full, and allowing the wort to splash a bit on the way in. Aeration at this stage will help the yeast grow so it can start to work quickly. When you're done siphoning, add the yeast, affix a fermentation lock to each container, and wait for fermentation to begin, usually in a matter of hours. You will see the yeast begin rising to the surface, followed by the formation of a head of foam. If you used the proper amount of yeast, your fermentation should be complete within a week in most cases. At that point, if visible signs of fermentation are over, take a sample for a specific gravity reading, and for tasting. It should taste like reasonably dry, flat beer, and be somewhat close to the expected final gravity.

Alternatively, allow the beer to ferment in the first container for four days. If the foam has dropped back to the surface, gently add the rest of the boiled and cooled water to a second five-gallon glass jug, and siphon the beer in as well, taking care to avoid splashing. The jug should be filled up into the neck. If not, add more water. Let the jug stand three or four days to allow further settling, and then bottle.

Personally, I prefer the second method, because moving the beer off the settlings an extra time seems to leave less sediment behind in the bottom of my bottles. The trade-off is that the first method involves one less processing of the beer.

With either method, you may substitute a covered plastic bucket for the glass jug as your fermentation container (but not for the settling tank in method two). These tend to be less expensive, though harder to sanitize due to the porosity of polyethylene. If using a bucket with a tight fitting lid, drill a hole in the lid so a fermentation lock can be attached. You may also substitute the new-style plastic water bottles for the glass jugs of either method. Also, there are occasionally some used acid jugs around with a capacity of between 6½ and 7 gallons. If you can find one, it will make an excellent fermentor because you can add all the water to the batch at once in the beginning.

There are two fermentation systems I strongly recommend against. First is the traditional stoneware crock. They are traditional and aesthetic, but they're also breakable, expensive, and too heavy to lift when filled. Also, unless the interior surface is absolutely perfect, it is possible for beer to penetrate into the ceramic, turn moldy, and infect subsequent batches.

Also, a few years ago a fermentation system, called the "Burton Union System," was being recommended by a number of people. It was a legitimate attempt to adapt a commercial technique to home brewing. With this system, the beer was fermented in a five gallon, glass jug, but the jug was filled completely up into the neck, and rather than a fermentation lock, a hose was attached, leading from the top of the jug to a bucket of sanitizing agent. The hose allowed gas, etc., to escape. I always considered this system too dangerous to recommend,

and in fact, I know of several cases where people clogged the opening
somehow, and blew up their jugs. I also know of a few other cases
where vapors from the bucket backed up through the hose into the jug,
rendering the beer undrinkable. Fortunately, even the people who first
introduced this system to home brewing have now abandoned it in
favor of a system like the one recommended here. However, you're
likely to find references to the Burton Union System in the home
brewing literature for some time to come, which is the reason I felt it
should be discussed here.

5. A Large Stirring Spoon. Stainless steel is best.

6. Fermentation Locks. You will need a fermentation lock for each
jug-type fermentor, as well as any bucket fermentor using a tightly
fitting lid. They are also called "air locks" or "bubblers," and are
available through any winemaking or brewing supplier. The inexpen-
sive, plastic, cylindrical type is probably best because it's the easiest to
clean. The fermentation lock is partially filled with water so that the
bottom of the interior sleeve will remain covered at all times. When
you are fermenting in a refrigerator with the cooling element at the top,
vodka should be used instead of water so the lock won't freeze solid.
Wine jugs with standard screw-top threads can be fitted with a screw-
top holder for the lock. Other gallon jugs will normally take a drilled
#6 rubber stopper. Most glass five gallon "water bottles" will use a
#6½ or #7 stopper. Unfortunately, there is variation, even among
these common jug types, so if you have a jug at home, measure the
diameter of the opening before shopping for a lock and stopper. It may
save you a trip to the store.

7. A Siphon Assembly. You will, at some point, need to siphon your
brew from one container to another. A five or six foot length of clear,
plastic, ⅜" i.d. hose with a stiff, "racking tube" attached to the
incoming end and a hose clamp near the other makes an excellent
setup. The stiff tube keeps the hose from curling up as it goes to the
bottom of the container you're siphoning from. Note that, from the
time fermentation begins, all the way up until your brew is in the
bottles, you should avoid mixing any more oxygen into it. Therefore,
make sure your hose goes all the way to the bottom of the container
you're siphoning into so splashing is minimized. This is still true at
bottling time, which is one reason you may wish to consider the option
of a bottle filler, a device which will be discussed later.

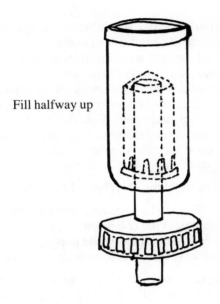

Fill halfway up

FERMENTATION LOCK

8. Bottles. Get good, cappable bottles of brown or green glass.
Avoid clear glass bottles as these afford no protection against the
effects of light. Exposing beer to either direct sunlight or flourescent
lighting can severely damage it, giving the beer a distinctly skunky
smell (Think about the flourescent lights next time you look at the beer
display in your local liquor store). Brown bottles afford your beer the
best protection, and green less (though more than clear). The trade-off
is that it's easier to see the fill level in green bottles than with brown
bottles when you're bottling, so you'll have to make your own decision
based on your circumstances. Even if you have flourescent lights in
your brewery, if the filled bottles aren't stored with direct exposure,
green bottles may be used. In any case, get the sturdiest bottles
possible that take a crown cap. Generally, deposit bottles are stronger
than no-deposit ones, though this is not always true.

Another consideration is the size of the bottles. Large bottles make bottling easier. However, bottle conditioned beers contain sediment, and tipping the bottle back upright will stir up an unnecessary amount of it. Therefore, don't use bottles larger than you intend to pour at one time. If you like large bottles, and can no longer find cappable quart bottles in your area, note that most domestic champagne bottles are designed to take a crown cap, and being $\frac{4}{5}$ quart, they are quite useful.

Over the years, I've had a few people tell me that they reseal screw-cap bottles with good success, but the majority complain that they lose at least some seals.

9. A Bottle Brush. Helpful in the recycling of old bottles.

10. A Carboy Brush. This is a large brush, long enough to reach the bottom of the jug, and bent near the end so the jug's shoulders can be cleaned. You may not need one of these while making your first brew, but you'll probably find it essential in getting ready for your second.

11. A Capper and Caps. Cappers come in a wide variety of styles. Get one that is durable, and that will work on the type of bottles you intend to use. Not all cappers will accept all bottles. If you wish to use champagne bottles but find your capper won't take them, purchase plastic champagne stoppers and wires from your supplier and tie them down as you normally would for champagne.

Crown caps have a seal on the under side either made of plastic or cork. Not much can go wrong with plastic lined caps, but cork hardens over time. This means it can't be easily compressed against the bottle lip to make a seal. You don't see cork lined caps that often these days, but should you run into some, you might want to use a few at first to make sure they seal. If you use cork lined caps and find some or all of your bottles failing to carbonate, the caps would be a good bet as a culprit. The ceramic-topped bottle has made a comeback in recent years, and can be used by home brewers. If you use them, however, you will need to replace the rubber gaskets from time to time.

OPTIONAL EQUIPMENT

In addition to the basics, there are a number of items you will probably want to acquire along the way. They all have a contribution to make relative to ease, precision and quality.

1. A Spare Refrigerator. In some climates, and certainly for classic lagers, this item should be moved from this list to the preceding one, unless you are so fortunate as to have an appropriately cold facility so fermentation and lagering at the required temperatures can be handled some other way. Some brewers cool their fermentations by putting their fermentors inside larger buckets and surrounding them with cold water. In hot climates, you can add ice if necessary. However, a refrigerator makes cooling the fermentation easier and somewhat more exact.

2. A Wort Chiller. The time when wort is being cooled after boiling, and before fermentation begins, is the time during the entire process when beer is most subject to infection. It is, therefore, important to accelerate the cooling process and get the yeast going as quickly as possible.

Probably the easiest and least expensive method is to take the covered boiling kettle, set it in a bathtub filled with cold water, turn on the faucet, and run cold water around it.

The second method is to use a wort chiller. There are a couple of styles which can be bought or built. The best is the "single tube" type which consists of about 40 feet of ½ inch copper tube coiled up with brass, male and female, garden hose fittings on the ends. Hoses are attached to run cold water from the nearest source through the coil while it sits in the boiling kettle, and back out to a drain. In this way you can usually add yeast within minutes of the end of the boil. The chiller is sanitized by setting it in a pail of chlorine solution, and especially by boiling water. Don't worry about the inside of the tube, because only water touches that. That's the advantage over the other "counterflow" type. With the counterflow chiller, the wort is siphoned through a copper tube. The tube has a larger hose outside it, through which cold water is pumped in the opposite direction. Unfortunately, counterflow chillers are more complicated to build, and with the wort passing through the inside of the tube, this kind of chiller can only be sanitized by intense heat, or by pumping a sanitizing agent through the copper tube from the bottom up.

3. A Wine Thief or Bulb-Type Baster. You sometimes need a way to extract samples. One of these will help.

4. A Scale. You'll probably want a scale sooner or later, because such things as hops are very difficult to measure without one. I recommend a small balance scale, the kind that has no springs to wear out.

5. pH Papers. These are for determining the acidity of your wort. If possible, get narrow range papers suitable for testing from around pH 4 to pH 7. You will probably be most interested in pH control if you decide to go on to advanced, grain brewing.

6. Draft Beer Equipment. Should you feel eliminating the work of bottling justifies considerable cash outlay, you may wish to investigate this option. Should you have access to an actual beer keg, you will need a carbon dioxide cylinder with a pressure gauge and faucet, and all the appropriate fittings.

A somewhat more common approach among home brewers is the use of five gallon, stainless steel, syrup dispensers, the type used for soft drink flavorings. These come in a variety of sizes and have handy, "quick disconnect" fittings. Neither type of keg arrangement comes cheap, but this system tends to be a bit less expensive.

There are also a number of plastic kegs manufactured in Britain, which tend to be quite a bit more reasonable in price. However, they are not designed for North American style carbonation. If, however, you're a fan of British ales, and don't mind low carbonation levels, you might look into them.

Of somewhat more promise, though not yet widespread, are some small plastic kegs made in West Germany. They are currently available in the five liter size, and have the same dispensing system as the large (about the same size) cans of German beer which began being marketed here some years back.

7. A Bottle Filler. The most common type is a tube that fits into one end of your siphon hose. At the bottom is a spring valve which opens when pressed onto the bottom of a bottle and closes when the pressure is withdrawn. A filler helps eliminate both messes and oxidation at bottling time. There are two kinds currently on the market, an aluminum one and a plastic one. The aluminum one fills a bit slower, but the plastic one creates more foam.

8. A Bottle Washer. Similar in principle to the bottle filler, this device attaches to a garden hose or a threaded faucet. It's a wonderful aid in rinsing out bottles.

9. Mashing and Sparging Equipment. The majority of home brewers will probably always brew using malt extracts and dry malts, rather than relying on grains alone for their fermentables. Most brewers, however, agree that their beers are improved by adding a small amount of grains for an extra freshness of flavor. With some recipes it's essential to get particular effects.

If using small amounts of the lighter grain malts along with your extracts, all you need is a pot to steep the cracked grains in, something to sprinkle or pour hot water with, and a colunder to hold the grain and allow the steeping (mashing) water and the rinsing (sparging) water to pass through into the boiling kettle below.

If you go on to advanced, all-grain brewing, then you will need a somewhat more specialized system, because you're relying solely on grains for all of your sugar (and eventually) alcohol. Special equipment for this type of brewing is discussed in the section on advanced brewing beginning on page 56.

10. A Grain Mill. If you do go on to work with large amounts of grains, you may well wish to invest in a grain mill. A "Corona" grain mill can be adjusted to give a coarse enough grind to work quite well. You will find the model with the large hopper most convenient, and I've known brewers to connect them to a ½ inch electric drill for convenience.

11. Cheesecloth or Straining Bags. In some situations, you may find cheesecloth or a nylon straining bag useful in straining out either grains or loose hops. Hops or black grains can be tied up in something like this when added to the boil. It helps with removal later.

12. A Dextrocheck® Kit. You will want to use every weapon at your disposal to determine if your beer is ready to bottle. This will normally include checking to see if there are still bubbles rising in the jug, reading your saccharometer, and tasting the test sample to see if it is dry or sweet. You may, however, find yourself uncertain even after all these steps. In this event, a Dextrocheck Kit will allow you to test directly for the amount of fermentable sugar remaining in your beer. By effecting a color change in the sample, this kit will show you the exact percentage of sugar present. One percent sugar, would be equal to four specific gravity points.

Dextrocheck also allows you to "cheat" if you have a beer just finishing fermentation and you have to leave on a trip. Because one percent sugar (four S.G.) is a normal amount of priming sugar to add to a batch, you can easily figure out how much to reduce your priming sugar so you can bottle before you leave. For example, let's say your test shows .5% residual sugar. Because you would normally bottle with ¾ cup of priming sugar in a five gallon batch, and your test shows half that amount already present, you may cut your addition in half, bottle, and safely leave on your trip. Some brewers have been known to rely on the Dextrocheck Kit exclusively for determining when to bottle and how to prime. The only reason not to is the expense of the kit.

INGREDIENTS

At least as important as the equipment you select are the ingredients which comprise the beer itself. Vast improvements have been made in this area in the last several years. This creates a particular need to discuss ingredients and what they do. For convenience, we can group them into six categories: malts, sugars and other adjuncts, hops, yeasts, water and water treatment, and optional refinements.

1. Malts. We could group malts and sugars together as "fermentables," for both provide sugars for the yeast to convert. Malt, however, is a far more complex subject than are the other sugars, and there is a considerable difference in the way it is treated. Malt exists at the very heart of brewing, for the malty flavors coming from malts combine with the bitterness and aromatic qualities of hops to form the foundation on which a given beer is built. Also, body, or more correctly, "full mouth feel," stems, at least partially, from the way the malt is handled.

Most sugars, on the other hand, serve primarily to raise the alcohol level in a given brew while doing relatively little for the body and flavor. Thus, if you prefer full-bodied, richly flavored beers, you will doubtless want to try brews with a relatively high malt content, severely limiting or eliminating the use of other sugars, except at bottling time.

Though other grains can be malted, most home brewers use the term "malt" primarily in reference to malted barley. In the malting process the grain is allowed to partially sprout. Then it is kiln-dried at lower or higher temperatures, depending on whether a light or dark colored malt is desired. Malting begins the process by which the starches in the grain are converted into fermentable sugars. The "mashing" procedure, in which the grain is crushed, water is added, and the mixture is steeped at particular temperatures for specified periods of time, completes the process.

Fortunately, home brewers don't need to go through all that to brew excellent beers. Reasonably priced, high quality, concentrated extracts of barley malt are on the market in either syrup or powdered form. These are concentrated from malt after it has been mashed, so beginning home brewers are able to brew a bit more simply than would otherwise be the case. For ease in differentiation, I call the concentrated syrups, "malt extracts" and the powdered extracts, "dry malts."

Up to this point, the best quality malt extracts and dry malts have been those from Britain, with a few good ones coming from Canada,

Germany, and Australia. However, now that home brewing has been
legalized in the U.S., it's very probable that top quality domestic malt
extracts will start to come on the scene. If so, by all means submit
them to exhaustive research.

In any case, light, amber, and dark malt extracts of good quality
may now be obtained, and some of the better known British brand
names have become household words among the American home
brewing fraternity.

Adding modest amounts of malt grains and/or other grains helps to
provide additional color or complexity of flavors. To do this, follow
the "Simple Infusion Mashing" procedure on pages 44–46 if using
Pale, Lager, Munich, Wheat, Mild Ale, or Crystal malts. The black
grains (Chocolate Malt, Black Patent Malt or Roasted Barley) are
added directly to the boiling kettle halfway through the boil. A number
of malt grains are now available to home brewers.

Pale Malted Barley will be referred to in just about any home
brewing text you happen to be reading. A distinction should be drawn,
however, between British and American pale malts. British pale malt
will be a bit darker, tending to give your beer a gold color. It also has a
somewhat different flavor than the American. Domestic pale malt
should properly be called Lager Malt.

Lager Malt is extremely light in color, crisp and dry in flavor. If
you advance to grain brewing, you will find yourself using it, logically
enough, as the base malt for making your very light, delicately
flavored lagers. Either Pale or Lager Malt can be used in small
amounts to add body and flavor to any type of beer, or to raise slightly
the Specific Gravity of a wort. They are also the primary malts used in
beers made "from scratch" by advanced brewers.

Mild Ale Malt has a bit more color than pale malt, and may be
substituted for it when making brown ales.

Munich Malt is a pleasant, aromatic malt, giving beer a gold to
amber cast, depending on the amount used. In many recipes you may
substitute it for Pale, Lager, or Crystal Malt for a somewhat different
effect.

Wheat Malt, added in small amounts will give your beer a light,
clean taste. It is also good for head retention.

Crystal (caramel) Malt is kiln-dried at a higher temperature than are
the above malts, and this gives it its darker color and caramelized
flavor. It is used in relatively small amounts for adding color and flavor
to amber, brown, and dark beers.

It should be noted that the term, "crystal malt," could cause confusion if you're reading American commercial literature. When professional brewers in this country use the term, they're speaking of a somewhat different malt. What we call "Crystal Malt" they call "Caramel Malt." This is because American home brewing has its roots in England, where the term, "Crystal Malt" is used, so this designation has become universal among home brewers, with most suppliers using it in their packaging as well. For this reason I'll stick with it.

Black Patent Malt is very dark and strong flavored. It is used in dark beers and stouts. Unlike the lighter grain malts, black grains do not have to be mashed, as all the starch has been effectively burned out during the kilning, and they consequently have little effect on the amount of fermentables in your wort. Unless you have a recipe indicating otherwise, add black patent malt, and the other black grains, to the boil uncrushed. If experimenting, start with small amounts and increase the ratio in successive batches until you find the level that best suits your taste. Used with restraint, these grains can yield good results, but they should be crushed only by the masochistic until some experience has been gained.

Roasted Barley is similar to Black Patent, but is roasted without being malted first. As Roasted Barley is used in Guinness Stout, it should be used in your Irish stouts as well. Technically, it is an adjunct, and it's placed here because it's usage is similar to that of Black Patent and Chocolate malts.

Chocolate Malt is given a slightly lighter roast than either Black Patent or Roasted Barley, and consequently has a bit less color, and a smoother flavor suitable for porters. You may, of course, experiment with these black grains, blending them in various proportions to suit your own taste.

Other specialty malts besides these may become available in the future, but at this point only one more needs mentioning.

Dextrine Malt, also known as cara-pils or cara-crystal, when added to a mash, contributes primarily unfermentable dextrins, increasing the full mouth feel of the beer, giving it additional smoothness and some-times a sense of sweetness as well. Dextrins are perhaps best under-stood by thinking of them as neither a sugar or a starch, but existing somewhere in between the two groups. They are not considered directly fermentable, though some yeasts may convert them to a fermentable form over an extended period of time. Dextrins are also formed in an ordinary mash, but the addition of up to a pound of dextrine malt to the mash for a five gallon batch of beer, allows you to increase the amount. Extract brewers can get a similar effect by adding dextrin in powder form.

Dextrin powder is relatively new to home brewers, though dextrins have always played a part in brewing. When grain malt is mashed, there are two kinds of enzymes at work. One kind converts grain starch into maltose, a fermentable sugar, while the other major enzyme creates dextrins, not directly fermentable, but giving the brew a kind of fulness and a sweet overtone. The first group of enzymes works most effectively at temperatures of 130–135 F. (55–57 C.) The second operates best at 150–158 F. (66–70 C.). If you were brewing from grain, you would vary your mash temperature to create the desired effect. Until recently, though, extract brewers have had their hands tied because most malt extracts are designed for a standard ratio of fermentability. The use of powdered dextrin allows you to vary things by creating a fuller, sweeter brew, just as using corn sugar or rice syrup allows you to move toward the lighter, drier, American style. If you wish to experiment with dextrin powder, use one or two ounces per five gallons with lighter, more delicate beers, ranging up to eight ounces in heavy, dark beers.

Dextrin powder is added during the boiling of the wort. Note that some "malto-dextrin" products contain only 30% dextrin, and 70% fermentable sugar. If not using 100% dextrin, adjust the amount accordingly.

2. Adjuncts. Simply expressed, the fermentation process is yeast cells acting on sugars present in the wort, dividing them into roughly equal parts of alcohol and carbon dioxide. Thus the amount of sugar present determines the final alcohol content. In brews where only malt is used, all the alcohol is derived from malt sugar (maltose). In others, when a lighter bodied, less malty beer is desired, or to accomplish particular effects, other sugars may be used to supplement the malt. These other sugars, as well as the grains and other things they are derived from, are known collectively as "adjuncts." Normally, at least 70% of the sugars in your wort will be derived from malt, and no more than 30% from adjuncts.

Corn Sugar (Dextrose) is the sugar most extensively used in home brewing. It is readily fermentable and carries less potential for off-flavors than cane sugar. The more sugar you substitute for malt in your beer, the lighter in color and taste the beer will be. If you wish to do a relatively light bodied, American style beer, you may use as much as 30% sugar. Note that either corn or cane sugar in large amounts may give your beer a "cidery" taste. If you find this disagreeable, stick to beers with a high malt content, using little sugar, or substitute rice syrup pound for pound of dry sugar.

Cane Sugar (Sucrose) will produce a slightly higher gravity, and consequently more alcohol, than corn sugar, but it has a hotter taste when fermented, making it less useful in brewing, particularly as far as the more delicately flavored beers are concerned.

Milk Sugar (Lactose) is non-fermentable, and can therefore be used to sweeten certain stouts. Lactose does this well, but it has a distinct flavor that doesn't go well with lighter beers. To add smoothness or a hint of sweetness to those beers, use dextrin powder (see p. 26). Lactose is best added by cooking up a sugar syrup just as you do with priming sugar, though it will not clarify quite as well.

Brown Sugar (or Molasses) can be used in small amounts for flavoring dark ales.

Rice Syrup is one of the more interesting adjuncts to come along recently. Some major American breweries use rice as an adjunct to lighten their beers. Rice tends to give beer a crisper, drier flavor than corn does, but until recently you could only use it by first boiling the rice, and then mashing it with barley malt (for enzymes). Rice syrup, however, may be added directly to your boiling kettle, just as you would with malt extract. This means you no longer have to be an advanced "all-grain" brewer to incorporate the flavor profile rice can give your beer. Note that beers made with rice syrup may take a bit longer to clarify in the bottle than other beers. To use rice syrup, substitute it for corn sugar on a pound for pound basis. You'll probably want to use corn sugar for priming, though, because its a lot easier to measure exactly.

There are a number of unmalted grains you may wish to experiment with. The easiest to work with are usually those in flaked form, because the flaking process prepares the starch for conversion to fermentable sugars when exposed to the enzymes present in barley malt. Because they don't furnish the enzymes themselves, the following adjuncts should always be mashed with an equal or greater amount of lager or pale malt.

Flaked Rice can be used in place of rice syrup, but the products I've seen have been prone to rancidity, so make sure it is fresh. As with the syrup, and with corn sugar, no more than 30% of the fermentable sugar should be derived from this source.

Flaked Oats can be used if you wish to try your hand at oatmeal stout. Use no more than a pound in a five gallon batch.

Flaked Wheat helps with head retention, and provides a bit of grainy character. I would use no more than 8 oz. in a five gallon batch.

Flaked Maize (Corn) or Yellow Corn Grits may be used in the same way and in the same amounts as flaked rice. The effect is slightly different.

Note that a number of potential adjuncts, including some of the ones just mentioned, are commonly available as breakfast cereals. If using these, read the label and be on the lookout for preservatives. You don't want to make things hard for your yeast, do you?

3. Hops. When brewers speak of hops, they refer to the flower cones of the female hop plant (humulus lupulus). It is these which are harvested, dried, and used in beermaking. Hops in this original flower form are usually called "whole hops."

Hops serve as a preservative, and as a flavoring and aromatic agent. It is useful to distinguish between "bittering" and "aromatic" hops, though in practice this distinction is somewhat obscured.

Bittering Hops are so designated because during the preparation of the wort they are boiled along with the malt for 60–90 minutes, during which time bitter resins are extracted from the hops, giving a pleasingly bitter flavor to the beer. This is the first major step if you are working with malt extract or dry malt, and the second (after mashing and sparging) if you are using grain. In practice, some of these hops are boiled the full time, and others are added a bit later. As the hops are boiled with the malt, the hop resins released into the wort afford a measure of protection against some potential contaminants.

In addition to whole hops, hop extracts in liquid form are frequently available. Used as directed, they may be substituted for all or part of your bittering hops.

A superior alternative, however, is the use of hop pellets, a relatively recent development with overwhelming commercial acceptance. These pellets, which look like rabbit food, are mechanically extracted from fresh hops, and therefore, retain the fresh hop flavor and aromatics exceedingly well. You use slightly less of these than with whole hops. I used to tell people to use 25% less with pellets than with whole hops. This was because a few years ago, hop packaging was not particularly good and whole hops in particular tended to be in bad shape, having lost part of their strength as well as their freshness. These poor conditions have changed recently with refrigerated or frozen storage, and/or oxygen barrier bag packaging. Consequently, whole hops have been staying in better condition, and I now consider an adjustment of 10% less for pellets a better estimate. Pellets are easy to use. They are stirred into the boiling wort in the same way as whole hops, but pellets do not need to be tied in cheesecloth. They disintegrate and the residue settles out during fermentation and storage.

Aromatic Hops play an important role in the making of almost any good brew. They are added to the wort at the end of the boiling process so that their fresh character is maintained. Their purpose is to add the glorious flavor and aroma of fresh hops to your beer. Choose your freshest and most aromatic hops for this purpose. Hop pellets may be used for your aromatic hops as well as bittering hops. It is true that a very slight loss of hop aromatics takes place during pelletizing, but the variety is more important than the form. If there is a choice, use pellets for bittering and whole hops for aromatics.

One of the most important developments in the past dozen years or so, is a major increase in the variety of available hops. A number of top grade varieties, both domestic and European, have become familiar to North American home brewers. As time goes by, the availability of specific types will probably vary, but here are some we've gotten to know.

Northern Brewer is a superb hop with a clean, almost minty flavor. It has roughly the same level of bitterness as Bullion or Brewer's Gold. This is my favorite hop for ales, stouts, and steam beers.

Cluster is a variety widely grown in the United States. It rates medium high in bitterness and has a characteristic taste which some home brewers don't particularly care for, but it serves acceptably as a bittering hop in blends. Early Cluster is the specific type most often available to home brewers. Late Cluster is somewhat less bitter.

Talisman is an improved cluster variety. It rates roughly the same as Early Cluster in bitterness. It is a top grade bittering hop.

Brewer's Gold is a strong, full-flavored hop, high in bitterness, suitable as a bittering hop in your most aggressive ales and stouts.

Bullion, a sister strain of Brewer's Gold, has very similar characteristics. They may be used interchangeably by the home brewer. This is, in fact, an extremely common practice in the brewing industry.

Fuggle has a spicy aroma, though it is quite low in bitterness. It's a good aromatic hop for ales and stouts.

Willamette is a strain of Fuggle grown in Oregon. Characteristics are similar.

Cascade is a somewhat mild variety with a distinctly floral aromatic quality. Used either as a bittering or aromatic hop in lager beers, Cascade blends well with Hallertauer and/or Styrian Golding.

Hallertauer, relatively low in bitterness, but with a crisp, spicy aroma, is probably my favorite aromatic hop for light lagers.

Tettnanger is, like Hallertauer, a German hop with similar flavor, but less aroma and may be substituted when available.

Styrian Golding is a spicy hop from Yugoslavia that blends beautifully into many lager beers.

Spalt is another German lager hop, not excessively bitter, but with a nice roundness of flavor. It blends nicely with any or all of the last four varieties mentioned. Used alone, it has the earthiness present in German varietals, without the spiciness of the Saaz.

Saaz is an assertive, Czechoslovakian hop considered by many the world's best. It is the backbone of Pilsner Urquell, considered by many the world's finest beer.

It should be mentioned that this list covers only the varieties currently available on the North American home brewing scene. New varieties are constantly being developed with the best of them going into commercial production. The trend is toward developing very bitter (high alpha acid) varieties. Three new varieties have emerged recently, Eroica, Chinook, and Nugget. If using one of these, use about 25% less than you would with Northern Brewer or Bullion, half as much as you would with Cascade.

The recipes in this book suggest particular varieties of hops. The selections reflect personal taste, and are in no way intended as definitive statements. Should you have other varieties where you are, try them out. The recipes are only intended as suggestions to get you started. With hops and malts particularly, you will no doubt want to start experimenting as soon as you have acquired a measure of experience and a degree of self-confidence. The recipes are good ones, but they've never been inscribed on stone tablets and hand caried down from Mt Sinai, at least so far as I know. Remember that one advantage of home brewing is the potential for arriving at your own personal beer, answerable only to your individual taste. As far as hops are concerned, just remember that more bittering hops will give you more bitterness, while more aromatic hops will increase the fresh hop flavor and aroma, and that some varieties are more bitter or more flavorful and aromatic than others (see pages 56–59).

4. Yeast. This, of course, is the living organism that makes the whole brewing process work. The yeast you use, therefore, should be selected with some care. The basic rule here is to use only a good quality, active beer yeast. Baker's yeast should only be used if there is absolutely no alternative. The fact that many old recipes call for it is inevitable, as it is only recently that beer yeast has become widely available. It is also true that beer yeast and baker's yeast descend from the same ancestral strain, S. Cerevisiae, and that both baker's yeast and ale yeast are still officially designated by this same term, but this is misleading. By means of mutation and selection over millions of yeast generations, the two industries have evolved yeasts vastly different in character. Beer yeast, for example, can be used in making bread, but it would probably take up to five or six times as long for the bread to raise. By the same token, baker's yeast, used in brewing, tends to ferment at an erratic pace, and often lends a strong, yeasty flavor to the beer. It settles out poorly, and that which does settle is easily disturbed when the beer is poured. Beer yeast can be purchased inexpensively enough that no one should still be sabotaging their product with an inferior yeast.

One more cautionary note is necessary. Brewer's yeast, as sold in bulk by health food stores, has been deactivated (killed) and will not work. Any fermentation you happen to get will stem from "wild" yeasts of undetermined character.

The topic of yeasts is a rather involved one. For example, I recall reading a few years back that there are 65 recognized sub-strains of lager yeast alone. By now there are possibly more. For our purposes, it will suffice to distinguish between ale yeast and lager yeast. These are commonly referred to as "top fermenting" and "bottom fermenting" respectively, though this distinction is often more traditional than accurate. Few, if any, dried ale yeasts are, in fact, true top fermenting yeasts. Bottom fermenting ale yeasts are often used for making ales commercially as well. A more meaningful distinction between ale and lager yeasts is that ale yeasts are generally hardier and more vigorous, but lager yeasts are hardier under cold conditions. Thus, ale yeasts should be used if fermenting above 65 degrees F. (16 C.), but lager yeast if fermenting below 55 degrees F. (13 C.). In between, you may use either.

There are, of course, likely to be some differences in the flavors produced by any two yeasts, not only between the strains, but within the classifications as well. This means you'll probably have to do some controlled experiments to see which you like the best. Personally, I like to make 10 gallon batches, split them up, and ferment with two different yeasts. Or you can do essentially the same thing by following the same recipe and procedure with successive batches, varying only the yeast.

It has always seemed to me that lager yeasts settle and stick to the bottom better than ale yeasts, but this may just be because lager beers are usually given more bottle time than ales, giving the "cake" a better chance to form.

One thing that should be stressed is that you should make sure to get what you pay for. "Beer Yeast," especially if packed in Britain, is almost certain to be an ale yeast. To be sure of getting a lager yeast, always look for the specific words, "Lager Yeast," or "S. Carlsbergensis" on the package.

Note also that yeast strains have a "maximum alcohol tolerance," and will stop working once the alcohol level gets to a certain point. The tolerance level varies, but for beer yeasts it is considerably below the level for wine yeast strains. To be safe, if you have a starting S.G. of 70 or above, switch to a wine yeast, preferably the "Pasteur Champagne" strain.

The majority of home brewers use dried beer yeasts, and there are some very good ones on the market. These are handy, generally have a good shelf life, and start readily when used at the rate of ½ ounce (14 grams) per five gallons of wort. Recently, several commercial quality, laboratory pure, liquid yeast cultures have found their way into home brew supply shops, and while these are relatively expensive, a number of them have proven to be excellent. Probably the number of such strains will increase significantly over the next few years, giving us increased flexibility. If using a liquid yeast culture, make doubly sure to aerate the wort by splashing it when putting it into your fermentor. Also, with liquid yeast cultures, you must make a yeast starter in advance.

A yeast starter is made up two to three days prior to boiling up your wort. Dissolve about 6 tablespoons of dry malt or malt extract in a quart of warm water. Add a pinch of yeast nutrient, heat to boiling, and boil for at least five minutes. When the mixture has cooled to around 80 degrees F. (27 C.), pour it into a small, sanitized jug, filling it no more than two thirds full. A 1.5 liter wine jug or magnum bottle is ideal for yeast starters.

Shake up your liquid yeast culture and add it to the jug. Attach a fermentation lock, and put the starter in a somewhat warm location, ideally between 70 and 80 degrees F. (21–27 C.), and leave it until it starts working actively. If more than four days go by under good conditions with no sign of action, pour off a bit and taste it. If it isn't sweet, it snuck past you while you weren't looking and is done. Should you have a starter ready, but something keeps you from brewing, put the starter in your refrigerator. You may keep it up to four days that way.

5. Water and Water Treatment. There are many types of water supplies, of course, and these will be variously suitable for brewing. Even an excellent brewing water will be better suited for making one type of beer than another. Generally speaking, brewing water should have a good clean flavor. If your supply is strongly flavored, you may decide to use bottled spring water for your brewing, partially or entirely. If you're a beginning brewer, that's probably all you should concern yourself with until you've made a few batches. Then come back to this. Within a given classification, the lighter the beer, the harder the water; with ales taking harder water than lagers. An exception is Czech-style pilsner, which is made with soft water, as are most black beers, including stouts and porters.

Water, obviously, is about as complex as any subject could be, but to start with, let's concentrate on understanding the three main types: permanently hard water, water high in "temporary hardness," and soft water. Another way of saying this is, "water high in sulfates, water high in carbonates, and water low in both." Those of you with a "municipal" water supply have it easy. You can simply call your water company and ask them which you have. In my area you can have a somewhat detailed printout sent just for asking. If you rely on a well, as I do, you'll have to figure things out for yourself.

The easiest way to distinguish between hard and soft water is to observe whether or not soapsuds form easily and profusely, a sign of soft water. As far as temporary hardness is concerned, look at your tea kettle. Waters high in carbonates or temporary hardness will precipitate a lot of "scale" when boiled.

In brewing, the general rule is that the lighter the beer, the harder the water used to brew it, with ales taking somewhat harder water than lagers. Of course, there has to be an exception, and that is Czech-style pilsner, which is made with very soft water.

As far as corrections are concerned, hardening soft water is the easiest. Simply adding a bit of Gypsum (calcium sulfate) normally does the trick. Calcium also helps give the yeast an extra boost. In the case of pale ales or British "bitters," you may also wish to add a very small amount of Epsom Salts (magnesium sulfate), no more than a third of a teaspoon for five gallons.

Very hard water is ideal for pale ales or bitters, but if you have that kind of water, you may have a hard time making some other types of beers at their very best. When you want to make darker brews, you may want to use some de-ionized water in the batch. The percentage you prefer will have to be determined by trial and error.

Water with high temporary hardness (carbonates) is not really desirable in most beers. Pre-boiling your brewing water, and siphoning it away from the precipitate will remove carbonates. Some temporary hardness is acceptable in stouts, porters, Munich style dark beers, bocks, and dopplebocks.

Soft water would be desirable for stouts, dark lagers, and Czech style pilsners. If you don't have soft water, you can sustitute partially with deionized water, available at grocers.

Small amounts of salt are added to many beers to give them smoothness and fullness. I recommend non-iodized salt, because I don't like adding anything, even in tiny amounts, that could tend to inhibit the yeast.

6. Optional Refinements. As you might expect, this is rather a catch-all, covering things which don't fit neatly into other categories, but which can be helpful nonetheless.

Yeast Nutrient, Food, Energizer, or Brewing Salts can be used to make your wort a more conducive medium for active fermentation. As the variety of names suggests, there are quite a few of these preparations available from various suppliers, and the precise formulations are as individual as the names. A teaspoon or so of one of these products, added prior to pitching the yeast, can help speed the onset of fermentation, and also help prevent "stuck fermentations," in which the yeast stops working before the job is finished.

Polyclar AT® (PVPP) is a proprietary product used to help precipitate unwanted proteins in all-grain beers. Add one gram per gallon to the fermentor just before siphoning in the wort, but at least 15 minutes before adding yeast. If yeast is present, it will cling to the Polyclar, keeping the protein away from it.

Irish Moss, actually a seaweed, is also used to get rid of proteins. It is added to the boiling kettle at the beginning of the boil to help with the "hot break," a coagulation and settling of unwanted protein. You probably won't need to worry about this until you begin using significant amounts of grain. I've seen two forms marketed; flaked, and powdered. Use about a teaspoon of the powdered, or a tablespoon of the flaked per five gallons of beer.

Ascorbic Acid (Vitamin C) is often added to beer after fermentation as an anti-oxidant. Half a teaspoon to five gallons is sufficient. Its purpose is to protect the beer against the air trapped in the bottle or aging tank. This is a particularly good idea if all or some of the beer will remain in storage for some time before being consumed. Note that only pure ascorbic acid should be used. Vitamin C tablets contain only small quantities of the pure stuff, supplemented with a lot of unknown buffers which could leave you with an insoluble, cloudy haze in your beer. This may be to your taste, but it's not to mine.

Sodium Erythorbate is another anti-oxidant on the market. It is used in the same manner and proportions as ascorbic acid.

Fining Gelatin and Grape Tannin may be used for a process called "fining," which some writers insist can give your beer more clarity than the unaided settling process can provide. Try it and see. To be honest, it's over twelve years since I've been tempted to fine my beer. In the first edition of *Quality Brewing*, I made fining an option since some other authors had made it a requirement. I've never been able to tell much difference.

At the point when you are putting your beer in the settling tank, stir a teaspoonful of unflavored gelatin (75 bloom: grade B) into 10–12 oz. of water (about one large water glass), and let it stand for a half hour. Siphon your beer into an open container. Heat the gelatin and water to 180 degrees F. (83 C.) and stir until the gelatin is dissolved. Stir it directly into the beer, and siphon the beer into a closed container for aging. The gelatin will combine with tannin, provided by the hops, and settle out impurities. Stirring in ¼ teaspoon of grape tannin before adding the gelatin can be beneficial to the process. The settling process will take approximately one week.

A Heading Agent may be used to give your brew a longer lasting head when poured than is otherwise possible. A number of such preparations have come into use by commercial breweries, especially since detergents, widely used for cleaning glassware, destroy the head retaining property naturally present in beer. Whichever heading agent your supplier stocks, use as directed.

PROCEDURES

If you chose to explore the earlier cross-references before continuing with your reading about equipment and ingredients, you will already be somewhat familiar with this section. You will also have begun to see that the "whats," the "whys," and the "hows" of home brewing are hopelessly interrelated. There is a process, of course, to match up with every ingredient and every piece of equipment. Some processes are self-explanatory. Others have already been clarified in the preceding two sections. A third group, however, requires more extensive comment, and to this group we now turn.

1. Cleaning. If you're a newcomer to winemaking or brewing, you probably think of cleaning the same way you would if you were washing dishes or canning jars. Boiling water, soaps, and detergents spring immediately to mind. None of these methods, however, should be applied to your brewing equipment or bottles. Boiling can soften plastic, crack crocks, and weaken glass bottles. Soaps and detergents can leave invisible residues, virtually impossible to rinse completely away, which could flavor your beer most unpleasantly, or interfere with its ability to form and hold a head.

Fortunately, when caring for your equipment, you have some better options. It is best to think of cleaning as a process distinct from sanitation. Cleaning refers primarily to everyday maintainance, the things you do to take care of your equipment after using it. At its simplest level, it involves nothing more than a lot of water. Anything you have just finished using, and which requires nothing more, is thoroughly rinsed off and allowed to dry. This includes your siphon hose, which can be cleaned by rinsing it off and then forcing water through it with a garden hose. It also includes your bottles. The second part of pouring a beer involves giving the bottle two or three good rinses with water, shaking them to dislodge any residual yeast. If you can, allow your containers to dry upside down.

There are, of course some non-routine cleaning situations. Any veteran home brewer will have encountered supplies of used beer bottles at some point in his career. Bottles are always nice to acquire, but they frequently contain layers of mold, cigarette butts, etc., and need appropriate attention. Also, fermentation containers may form a resinous, gummy layer around the surface of the fermenting beer. When soaking with water won't do the job, situations like these require extra measures.

A simple method of sparging small amounts of mashed grain, collecting the water in the boiling pot.

Adding the malt extract.

Gypsum and other water treatment items are added.

Hops are needed to round out the brew. In this case, hop pellets are being used.

The wort is boiled, stirring occasionally, and more hops are added at appropriate intervals.

The simplest and best kind of wort chiller is about 40 feet of half-inch copper tubing wound into a coil. Garden hose fittings are attached to the ends. The chiller coil is placed in the boiling kettle, and cold water is pumped through it as soon as the fire has been turned off.

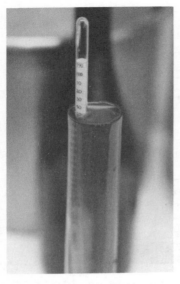

When the wort has cooled, a specific gravity reading is taken.

You're then ready to add the yeast or starter.

Five gallons of wort has been divided into two jugs, yeast has been added, and fermentation is actively underway. Foam and resinous materials find their way to the surface and gas escapes through the fermentation lock.

After fermenting for a few days, the beer is siphoned into a single settling tank which will be filled into the neck to allow a minimum of air exposure.

Settling, along with any remaining fermentation still needed, will take place over the next few days. The beer is then siphoned away from the sediment, primed, bottled, and set aside to carbonate.

A lock-lid bucket with a spigot can make sparging easy for all-grain brewers. A large nylon straining bag, held in place by the lid, keeps grain from clogging the spigot.

This is really what it's all about. The optimum time for savoring your beer, by the way, is while you're cooking up a new batch.

Chlorinated TSP (Tri-sodium phosphate) is my choice as a glass cleaner, because it works with either hot or cold water. Use one heaping tablespoon per gallon of water. If you are removing resins from a glass jug, fill the jug with this mixture and let it stand overnight. A quick and easy turn with a brush can then remove the loosened resins. Many bottles will respond to just 10 or 15 minutes in a sink of TSP and hot water. If not, leave the TSP mixture in the bottles and stand them aside for a day or two. After that, a quick brushing out will usually suffice. Rinse at least three times with clear water.

Soda Ash, used at the rate of ¼ cup per gallon, can also be used for cleaning, but only with hot water. For this reason, don't use it with large glass jugs. These are made of quite thick glass, and heating can crack them. It does work well, though, on brewing kettles and plastic containers. Soda Ash is generally somewhat less expensive than TSP. As with TSP, rinse at least three times with clear water.

"B-Brite" is worthy of mention as well. It is a proprietary product with hydrogen peroxide the active ingredient. Take an ounce for every 1½ to two gallons of hot water, and let the item to be cleaned soak for 15 to 30 minutes or longer. This product is marvelous for removing stubborn things like "beer stone," the deposit that forms on your boiling kettle after a few uses. It also does a great job on burnt spots on pot bottoms. "B-Brite" may be used with hot tap water, or you may fill the pot and heat it on the stove, even boiling it for awhile if necessary. Some suppliers may carry similar cleaners under other names.

2. Sanitation. It is not enough to make sure that your containers and utensils are clean. In most cases they must also be sanitized. The specific goal of sanitation is to eliminate wild yeast and bacteria from any contact with your wort or beer. Any utensil or container coming in contact with the brew after the boiling of the wort must be sanitized.

Chlorine is the most effective, readily available, sanitizing agent. A sink or bucket should be filled with water, and household chlorine bleach mixed in at the rate of two tablespoons per five gallons. After this mixture has been allowed to stand for ten minutes or so, it may be used to sanitize anything needing to be treated. Let objects to be sanitized stand in contact with the chlorine solution for 30 minutes and let them drain dry for a minute or two or shake them off. A solution of this strength will not flavor your beer if the sanitized item is still damp when used. Hoses can be sanitized by siphoning some of the solution and clamping off the flow to let the hose stand full for the required time. Bottles and carboys can be sanitized a few days ahead if they can be stored upside down until you're ready to use them. Inverted storage (Make sure case bottoms are clean.) will keep unwanted organisms from falling into your bottles until they're ready to be used. You may wish to make up a chlorine solution and keep it covered for incidental use. If so, change the solution once a week or so to retain its full effectiveness. If you are sloppy about sanitation, it's a good bet that it will catch up to you sooner or later. Winemakers are sometimes surprised that home brewers take such pains in this area, but beer has significantly less than wine of two things that tend to insure stability; alcohol and acid. Therefore, additional care is needed. It should be said, however, that it is possible, though less likely, to err in the other direction. I have seen some prospective brewers who were so terrified of contamination possibilities that they were literally afraid to process their beer, or to make beer at all. Less common than a tendency toward sloppiness, unreasoning fear is also a failing. I sometimes think beer, like a growling dog, can sense when it has someone intimidated. Remember that fermentation is a relatively straightforward process, and beer has been made for a lot longer than we've known anything about yeast or bacteria. Take reasonable care of your sanitation and I think you'll be happy with the results.

The British home brewers have traditionally used bisulphite or metabisulphite solutions for their sanitizing agents. As our North American tradition is directly descended from theirs, many of us followed their lead for years. However, these agents are not as effective against bacteria as chlorine, and they require rinsing which negates the sanitation. The reason "sulphites" are used in Britain is that their household chlorine bleach is perfumed, rendering it useless. This is potentially important because perfumed chlorine bleach has now been introduced in the U.S. as well, and should not be used.

Please note that "sulphite" is used in home winemaking in a number of contexts, and many brewers will have a jug of it around. Never allow these solutions to come in contact with chlorine. A potentially dangerous gas can be created if that happens.

3. Simple Infusion Mashing. Mashing is the cooking process which allows enzymes in the malt to finish converting grain starch to fermentable sugar. This conversion was begun when the grain was malted. Though the grain mashing process when beer is being made from scratch can become rather involved, it is not necessary to be too sophisticated when you are using only a pound or two of grain to add some grainy character to a batch of extract beer. The point, in this case, is not necessarily to extract every last gram of sugar from the grain, but to get some unique character (and sometimes color) into the beer. If your grain is uncracked, crack it in a grain mill, coffee grinder, or a slow-speed blender. Place the cracked grain in a pot and cover it with water. Cover the pot and set it in the oven with the thermostat set at 150 degrees F. (65 C.) and leave it there for 45 minutes to an hour. You can do this on the stove top as well, but you'll have to watch the temperature a bit more closely.

It will probably not be necessary with small amounts of grain malts, but should you get into advanced, all-grain brewing, or to the point where you're relying on a lot of grain in your batch, you will probably want to test your mash to see if all the starch has been converted. This is done as follows. Take a few drops of liquid from the mash, and place it in a white saucer or something similar. Take care not to pick up any pieces of the grain husk as you do so. Add a drop or two of red iodine to the liquid, and mix it in. If the liquid turns dark blue or black, starch is still present and the mashing must continue. If the iodine blends with it, essentially becoming colorless, all the starch has been converted and the mash should be stopped. Don't allow your mash to go on longer than an hour and a half, however. There won't be much, if any, enzyme activity left at that point, and you may begin to extract undesirable elements from the grain.

After mashing, the grain must be sparged or rinsed. Remove it from the oven and pour the mash water into your boiling pot through a strainer or colander. Pour hot water through the grain, rinsing (sparging) the grain as thoroughly as possible until the runoff is clear. Ideally, the sparging water should be between 150 and 165 degrees F. (66 to 74 C.) though hot tap water will suffice. Then discard the spent grain, add the other ingredients to the pot, and procede to boil the wort as you normally would. All of the lighter grain malts up through crystal malt should be mashed.

Should you have a situation you're not sure of, you may wish to add Koji or Diastase to the grain to insure complete starch conversion.

Koji (Aspergillus Oryzae) is an enzyme that converts grain starch to fermentable sugar. It is traditionally used in the conversion of rice for sake, but it can be very useful with barley malts as well. It may be added during the mash. Take a cup or two of water and stir in about half a tablespoon of Koji for each pound of grain used (1 Tbl. per Kilo). Hold the temperature of the entire mash at 130 degrees F. (54 C.) for 10 minutes before proceding to raise the temperature further.

The complex of enzymes contained in malt grains themselves, which effects the conversion of starches into fermentable sugars, is commonly known as "Diastase" or "Amylase." You may purchase this separately as well, and add it in the same manner as Koji. Half a teaspoon per pound of grain should suffice.

4. Lagering. If you are making a traditional style lager beer, it should be set aside after fermentation to age for a period of at least three weeks. At a brewery, this would normally be done in bulk, at about 32 degrees F. (0 C.). Lager beers take their name from this cold aging (lagering) process. During this time, a subtle change takes place in the beer as it gains smoothness and delicacy. This is in contrast to the more rough and ready ales and stouts, which may be consumed as soon as full, or sometimes even partial, carbonation has been achieved and the yeast has begun to drop to the bottom of the bottle. For grain brewers, lagering also helps precipitate the protein which causes "chill hazes," a phenomenon in which perfectly clear beers become cloudy when refrigerated.

Obviously, you have to have a spare refrigerator if you're going to lager your beers in bulk. Do not attempt it at warmer temperatures that will encourage bacterial growth. Unless you have refrigeration capacity, age your beer in the bottle, where the carbon dioxide will afford it some additional protection.

If you've been lagering for a number of weeks, add a pack of yeast at bottling time along with your priming sugar (in case your original yeast is no longer active).

5. Carbonation. Home brewed beers are carbonated by the time-honored method known as "bottle conditioning," in which a limited amount of fermentation is allowed to take place in the bottle. The objective of this fermentation is to produce and trap carbon dioxide, though there is a very slight increase in alcohol content.

Old-time, prohibition era, home brewers used to quickly bottle their still fermenting beer when the specific gravity dropped to the appropriate level. Unfortunately, this can be a bit tricky, unless you are quite experienced, and the desired point can be reached as easily at three a.m. as at any other time. Therefore, such varied results as flat beer, late night bottling sessions, or blown bottles and sticky messes, were relatively common. In fact, to this day, the exploding bottle remains probably the most widespread and enduring bit of American home brewing folklore. Such problems can, of course, be quite discouraging, not only to brewers themselves, but to those who share their households as well. Happily, they are easily avoided.

The simplest method of carbonating home brewed beer is to let the beer ferment completely out. Once the beer is flat, you can then "prime" it with a measured amount of sugar to give you just the right amount of carbonation. If your beer is being bottled within a few days after the end of fermentation, you should use approximately ¾ cup Corn Sugar to five gallons of beer. If your brew has been lagered, it will have had time to vent some additional trapped carbon dioxide left over from fermentation, and you may wish to increase the priming sugar to a full cup.

The best way to add priming sugar is to stir it into 1–2 cups of water. Heat to boiling, stirring occasionally, and boil for five minutes. Boiling turns the mixture into a syrup which will dissolve easily in the beer. Ascorbic Acid may be added to it as well. Siphon the beer off of its sediment into an appropriate container, add the sugar syrup, siphon the beer immediately into bottles, and cap them.

Should you taste a beer you're about to bottle and decide it needs some extra hop flavor and aroma, you may make a correction with an alternate priming method. Tie ¼ to ½ oz. of your freshest whole hops in cheesecloth and put them in 2 cups of water and boil from two to five minutes. Remove the hops, add your priming sugar, heat once again to boiling, and proceed as you normally would.

After you've gained some experience, you may wish to try the traditional priming method known as kraeusening, assuming the name hasn't scared you off. It simply means priming a finished beer by adding to it a small amount of a new wort which has just begun to ferment. Add enough wort to raise the gravity by 5 to 6 points. That should give you 4 points of fermentability or thereabouts.

Whichever priming method you use, your ales should be given 1–2 weeks in the bottle at cellar temperature. As clarity is generally considered more important for lagers, they should have 3–4 weeks minimum. When bottling a beer that has been lagering, add a pack of dry lager yeast, just to make sure the yeast is active.

6. Final Gravities. The higher the malt content of a given beer, the higher the final gravity will be. If you had a wort that had about a four to five malt to sugar ratio like many old-time homebrews, it would probably gravity all the way down to approximately zero (1.000). As the ratio of malt to sugar is increased, the final gravity you may expect also goes up in relatively direct proportion until, with an all malt wort, it reaches a point which is roughly one-fourth the starting gravity of the wort. Thus you may calculate the expected final gravity of most all malt worts by dividing the starting gravity by four.

All this may seem frighteningly complex, but it really isn't if you remember that your saccharometer doesn't measure sugar directly, but infers it by indicating the weight of a solution. In introducing the saccharometer, it was mentioned that sugar is heavier than water, but alcohol lighter. Therefore, if you were able to ferment a solution of pure, highly refined sugar, the gravity would start out above 1.000 and finish below it, down towards .990. Malt, however, is not so highly refined, and contains additional elements which provide body (and weight). Thus, more malt means more weight and a higher final gravity, but more alcohol derived from a refined sugar means the final gravity will be lower.

This should explain why beers with a higher sugar content should finish up closer to zero, while high malt beers terminate somewhat higher. By derivation, you should be able to see why you need to raise the gravity slightly more than the actual sugar content desired when kraeusening with high malt worts.

Note that a very black beer will probably finish a bit higher still. The reason a black grain, such as black patent malt, will cause this is that most of the fermentables were burned out of it when it was kilned. It can still add other elements to a wort, increasing the percentage of non-fermentables, and thereby raising the final gravity. In most cases, dividing the starting gravity by three will establish the upper limit of the final gravity range for these beers, though some stouts can go a bit higher. This will also be true, of course, for beers with a high dextrin content, either because of a high mash temperature (in the case of all grain beers) or because powdered dextrin has been added.

Obviously, you should look for the absence of visible signs of fermentation, and also taste the beer to see if any untoward sweetness remains. If you have serious doubts about whether a given batch is finished, get a Dextrocheck Kit (or something similar) and test to see how much residual sugar is left in the beer.

7. Serving. I can't tell you the optimum temperature at which to serve your beer, because that's something you have to decide. I will say, though, that over the years I've personally come to prefer my ales, porters, and stouts between 55 and 60 degrees F. (13–16 C.), and my lagers between 45 and 50 degrees F. (7–10 C.).

All home brewed beers have a tiny bit of sediment at the bottom of the bottle. There may be some who regard this as a minor annoyance, but I find it part of the beer's charm, a reminder of its natural origin. In any case, sediment is not particularly pleasant to taste, so your beer should be poured slowly into a tilted glass until the sediment approaches the lip of the bottle. Then tip the bottle upright again, not allowing any sediment to pass. As a skilled hand will waste very few drops of beer in the process, rigorous practice is suggested.

Sit back then, and enjoy the fruit of your labors. Such a moment combines the appreciation of good beer, the fulfillment of at least one of your creative urges, and the achievement of a bit more independence than is often possible in modern life.

8. Oxidation: A Cautionary Tale. Whenever you're moving your beer from one container to another at any stage in the beermaking process, you should take pains to expose it to as little oxygen as possible. This means making sure that splashing is minimized by having the hose go right to the bottom of the container you're moving the beer into. It also means making sure that settling and lagering containers are filled so that the air surface is kept to a minimum. Careless exposure of your beer to the air can severely affect its quality. Splashing is only desirable before your wort has begun to ferment. Oxygen at that stage is beneficial to yeast growth, and has no other harmful effects. This is most definitely not the case later.

PROCEDURE FOR LAGERS

The procedure for these beers differs in some respects from the procedure for ales and stouts. In general, it is a somewhat more sophisticated approach to brewing. Whether or not it is worth it to you to take the extra care necessary to produce true lager beers is a question each home brewer must answer for him or herself. Perhaps you will go all the way, with cold fermentation followed by a period of lagering (see p. 46), only for particular showpiece beers. The rest of the time, cool fermentation, followed by aging in the bottles at cellar temperatures, will be employed. Good beers may be made by either method, though most lager beers can be improved with the full treatment. Here is how to do lager beers.

Cooking

If your recipe contains Lager, Pale, Munich, Crystal or Wheat Malt, place the cracked or ground grain in a kitchen pan, cover loosely with water, heat to approximately 150 degrees F. (66 C.), cover and let stand (either on the stove top or in the oven) for 45 minutes to an hour.

Place a colander over your boiling kettle and pour in the grain, letting the water collect in the pot below. Rinse through the grain with hot water, at least 130 degrees F. (54 C.) but no hotter than 170 F. (77 C.), until a clear runoff is obtained. Discard the grain. The liquid becomes part of the boil.

If none of these malts are called for, omit the above steps, and go directly to the boiling of the wort as follows.

Thoroughly dissolve any of the following called for in your recipe: Malt Extract, Dry Malt, any Sugar except priming sugar, Rice Syrup, Dextrin Powder, Gypsum, Salt, Epsom Salts, Irish Moss, or Yeast Nutrient, in two or more gallons of water (as much as possible). Heat to a rolling boil. Stir in a quarter of the Bittering Hops and boil for 15 minutes. Stir in half of the Bittering Hops and boil for 15 more minutes. Add any black grains called for, and boil 15 more minutes. Stir in the remaining Bittering Hops and boil 15 more minutes, adding the Aromatic Hops, if called for, during the last two minutes of the boil.

After the end of the boil, the wort should be cooled as quickly as possible to a temperature between 70 and 85 degrees F. (21–27 C.), so the yeast can be added.

Fermentation

Siphon your cooled wort into one or more sanitized glass jugs, filling them no more than two thirds full. Add Yeast, attach a fermentation lock to each, and allow the fermentation to procede.

Fermentation for lager beers is essentially the same as for ales except the temperature should be kept colder and lager yeast is used. With dry lager yeasts, the ideal temperature is between 50 and 55 degrees F. (10 to 15 C.), though some commercial cultures (normally available in liquid form) may ferment down as low as 40 degrees F. (5 C.). As with the ales, if enough yeast is used and sanitation procedures are carefully followed, fermentation will normally be concluded in a week or less.

In five to seven days, when apparent yeast activity has ceased, the saccharometer reading is somewhere near where it's supposed to be, and the sample you're testing tastes like dry, flat beer, lagering is the next step.

Lagering

True lager beers must, naturally, be lagered. When fermentation has finished, siphon your beer into a second glass jug, topping it up with previously boiled and cooled water. Stopper up the jug and store the beer under refrigeration as close to 32 degrees F. (0 C.) as possible for at least three weeks. You might lager your beer for as long as three months, but you'll probably find the space in your refrigerator is more profitably used for lagering subsequent batches. Temperature is important, so don't try lagering unless you can at least get it down to 40 degrees F. (4 C.). Without that sort of control, you should bottle your beer at the end of fermentation, and age it in the bottles.

Bottling

When lagering is finished, siphon the beer away from the sediment, stir in half a pack of lager yeast along with your priming sugar syrup (see p. 47), siphon the beer into bottles and cap them. After a week or two, chill a bottle and try it. If enough yeast has dropped out so that the beer is clear, it is ready to drink. When that happens, immediately chill a couple more to sip while cooking up a new batch. This rigorously disciplined approach to home brewing will help maintain the proper level of inspiration, allowing you to get the most possible enjoyment from your chosen craft.

Lager Beer Recipes

1. American Style Lager—5 U.S. gal. (19 liters)

3 lbs. (1.4 kilos) Light Dry Malt
1 lb. (454 grams) White Rice Syrup or Corn Sugar
1 tsp. Gypsum
½ tsp. Salt
¾ oz. (21 grams) Bittering Hops (Spalt, Cluster, or Cascade)
¼ oz. (7 grams) Aromatic Hops (Hallertauer or Cascade)
Water to 5 gallons (19 liters)
¾ to 1 cup Corn Sugar for priming
½ oz. (14 grams) Lager Yeast

Starting S.G.   36
Final S.G.   6–8
Alcohol by vol.   3½%

2. North European Style Pils—5 U.S. gal. (19 liters)

4 lbs. (1.8 kilos) Light Dry Malt
1 lb. (454 grams) Lager Malt
4 oz. (113 grams) Munich Malt
1 tsp. Gypsum
¼ tsp. Salt
1¾ oz. (50 grams) Bittering Hops (Hallertauer)
½ oz. (14 grams) Aromatic Hops (Hallertauer)
Water to 5 gallons (19 liters)
¾ to 1 cup Corn Sugar for priming
½ oz. (14 grams) Lager Yeast

Starting S.G.   44
Final S.G.   11
Alcohol by vol.   4%

3. Czech Style Pilsner—5 U.S. gal. (19 liters)

4½ lbs. (2 kilos) Light Dry Malt
1½ lbs. (681 grams) Munich Malt
8 oz. (227 grams) Wheat Malt
2 oz. (57 grams) Black Patent Malt (added to boil)
2 oz. (57 grams) 100% Dextrin Powder (optional)
2½ oz. (71 grams) Bittering Hops (Saaz)
¼ (7 grams) Aromatic Hops (Saaz)
Water to 5 gallons (19 liters)
¾ to 1 cup Corn Sugar for priming
½ oz. (14 grams) Lager Yeast

Starting S.G.   50
Final S.G.   12–13
Alcohol by vol.   4¾%

4. Vienna Style Amber Lager—5 U.S. gal. (19 liters)

4½ lbs. (2 kilos) Light Dry Malt
2 lbs. (907 grams) Munich Malt
2 oz. (57 grams) 100% Dextrin Powder (optional)
1 tsp. Gypsum
½ tsp. Salt
1 oz. (28 grams) Bittering Hops (Hallertauer or Tettnanger)
Water to 5 gallons (19 liters)
½ oz. (14 grams) Lager Beer Yeast

Starting S.G.   47–48
Final S.G.   12–13
Alcohol by vol.   4¼%

5. Munich Style Dark—5 U.S. gal. (19 liters)

4 lbs. (1.8 kilos) Light Dry Malt
1 lb. (454 grams) Munich Malt
8 oz. (227 grams) Crystal Malt
4 oz. (227 grams) Black Malt (added to boil)
2 oz. (57 grams) 100% Dextrin Powder
1½ oz. (43 grams) Bittering Hops (Hallertauer and/or Spalt)
Water to 5 gallons (19 liters)
¾ to 1 cup Corn Sugar for priming
½ oz. (14 grams) Lager Yeast

Starting S.G.   50
Final S.G.   15
Alcohol by vol.   4¼%

6. Bock—5 U.S. gal. (19 liters)

3½ lbs. (1.6 kilos) Amber Malt Extract
2 lbs. (907 grams) Light Dry Malt
4 oz. (113 grams) Munich Malt
4 oz. (113 grams) Crystal Malt
8 oz. (227 grams) Chocolate Malt (added to mash)
4 oz. (113 grams) 100% Dextrin Powder
½ tsp. Gypsum
¾ tsp. Salt
1½ oz. (43 grams) Bittering Hops (Tettnanger)
½ oz. (14 grams) Aromatic Hops (Hallertauer)
Water to 5 gallons (19 liters)
½ oz. (14 grams) Lager Yeast

Starting S.G.   55
Final S.G.   15
Alcohol by vol.   5%

7. Dopplebock—5 U.S. gal. (19 liters)

6½ lbs. (3 kilos) to 7 lbs. (3.2 kilos) Light Malt Extract
2 lbs. (907 grams) Munich Malt
1½ lbs. (681 grams) Crystal Malt
6 oz. (170 grams) Chocolate Malt (added to boil)
2 oz. (57 grams) Black Patent Malt (added to boil)
8 oz. (227 grams) 100% Dextrin Powder or 4 oz. (113 grams) Lactose
½ tsp. Gypsum
¾ tsp. Salt
1½ oz. (43 grams) Bittering Hops (Eroica)
1 oz. (28 grams) Aromatic Hops (Cascade or Hallertauer)
Water to 5 gallons (19 liters)
½ oz. (14 grams) Lager Yeast

Starting S.G.   65
Final S.G.   25
Alcohol by vol.   5%

A SHORT INTRODUCTION
TO ADVANCED BREWING

If you're a beginning brewer, you should probably stop reading at this point until you've made a few batches. Then come back and go on. If you try to absorb too much information all at once, you could get confused. Likewise, if this is the only book on home brewing you have read, do some brewing before reading another. Don't read too many at once. Another writer may have a different method, and both may work fine, but not together. With a little experience you should have no trouble figuring out what you can most comfortably take from one source, and what from another. There will be plenty of time to add to your knowledge, and you should, but after all, making beer is more fun than reading about it.

Formulating Your Own Recipes

This is not particularly difficult, and you'll undoubtedly want to give it a try. As a general guideline, I would suggest a minimum of 3 lbs. of malt extract and a maximum of 1½ lbs. of corn sugar or other adjuncts in a five gallon batch.

Hops, of course, may be increased or decreased according to taste. You may also change varieties, or blend a number of types, to achieve particular effects. The subject of hops can be complex. The amount of alpha (lupulic) and beta (lupulinic) acids present determines the potential bitterness in any given hops with alpha acids accounting for most of it. Consequently, hop bitterness is normally rated in terms of the alpha acid content. The amount of essential oils determines the degree of aromatics. The particular variety you are using determines the type of flavor and aroma you will get. I can't predict the specific hop varieties and harvests you'll encounter in the future, but here are the best figures available for the more commonly available types, showing average alpha acid contents. You may find the table useful when changing varieties for a given recipe, or when blending several types for extra complexity.

Hop Alpha Acids by Variety

Variety	% Alpha
Brewers Gold	8–10
Bullion	8–10
Cascade	5–7
Cluster	7–9
Comet	9–10
Eroica	11–13
Fuggle	4–6
Galena	12–14
Golding	4–6
Hallertauer	4–6
Hersbrucker	4–6
Northern Brewer	8–10
Nugget	12–14
Saaz	5–6
Spalt	4–5
Styrian Golding	6–7
Talisman	7–9
Tettnanger	5–6
Willamette	6–8

Note that these figures are only averages. There is a trend in the home brew trade toward labelling hop packages with the alpha acid rating of the specific lot. This is a helpful practice, and should be encouraged. With this information, and the following chart, you should be able to be much more exact in your brewing, especially if you are using hop pellets. It will work with loose hops too, though these are subject to more variation in small lots.

Hop Bittering Units for Common Beer Types (in 5 gallons)

Type	B.U.
American Lager	10–15
Pils	23–35
Pilsner	25–26
Oktoberfest/Maerzen/Vienna	18–29
Munich Dark	14–24
Bock	25–28
Dopplebock	24–30
Pale Ale	20–55
Bitter	30–55
Alt	24–29
Brown Ale	13–23
Porter	20–65
Dry Stout	40–75
Sweet Stout	70–113
Imperial Stout	100–135
Barley Wine	65–135

This chart can help determine the proper amount of hops to use in a particular type of beer. It may be used in two ways.

First, if you have some hops, and know the alpha acid rating, you can figure their bittering value in five gallons of beer by getting out your calculator and going through a few basic steps as follows:

(A) Multiply the number of ounces of hops (per five gallons) by their alpha acid rating (percent alpha acid).

(B) Divide the result by 7.25.

(C) Multiply the result by one of the following figures, depending on the length of time the hops are boiled. If the hops are boiled 45 minutes or longer, multiply by 28–30. If the hops are boiled 15 to 40 minutes, multiply by 8–12. If the hops are boiled less than 15 minutes, or are dry hopped, multiply by 5. The answer gives you the number of bittering units. Note that a quick chilling of the wort at the end of the boil is presumed. If the hops steep in hot water past the end of the boil, additional time must be figured in to your calculations. Note also that, if you add your hops in stages, you will have to go through these steps separately for each addition.

Here's an example of how to use this information. Let's say you have 2 oz. of hops in the house, you would like to make five gallons of porter, and you can't get to the home brew supply shop for several days. Your hops have an alpha acid rating of five percent, so you start by multiplying the number of ounces by the alpha acid rating, and proceed as follows:

(A) 2 oz. times 5 alpha = 10.

(B) 10 divided by 7.25 = 1.38.

(C) 1.38 times 29 (figuring an hour's boiling time for all the hops) = 40.02 bittering units. Looking at the chart, you see that 40 bittering units is fine for a porter, so you may go ahead and brew.

It can also be very useful to work these calculations in reverse. For example, let's say that you went ahead, made your porter, and decided 40 bittering units is exactly what you want in that type of beer. However, when you buy hops for another batch, you find your supplier has gotten in a new lot with an alpha acid percentage of seven. Your task is to find out how many ounces of hops it will take to give you 40 bittering units in five gallons of brew. This is what you do:

(A) Figuring an hour's boiling time, as before, divide 40 by 29 (40 divided by 29 = 1.38).

(B) Multiply the result by 7.25 (1.38 times 7.25 = 10.005).

(C) Divide the result by the percent alpha acid in the hops (10.005 divided by 7 = 1.43). Therefore you would need 1.43 ounces of these hops to equal the 40 bittering units obtained from a full two ounces of the others.

This procedure will probably seem complicated at first, but the reward for mastering it is greatly improved consistency in your brewing.

The bittering units used here are calculated according to the American Society of Brewing Chemists' (ASBC) system. *Zymurgy* magazine uses a simplified system of "homebrew bittering units." Multiply the number of homebrew bittering units (HBU) by three to get the equivalent number of ASBC bittering units. Likewise, divide the ASBC units by three to figure the HBU.

Introduction to All Grain Brewing

A percentage of you will eventually want to go on and try your hand at advanced, all-grain brewing. Those who do go on will do so, at least partially, because this is how beer is made by most commercial breweries, and the challenge is irresistible. Others will do so because some beers, notably the more delicate, light beers, are most easily made from grain. In general, this will be true if a fresh grain aroma is a significant part of the beer's charm.

Should you feel, as I do, that the satisfactions derived are sometimes worth the extra time and effort involved, this brief introduction will help to get you started, though a number of publications have now been written about advanced brewing, and you'll undoubtedly want to read further. When you do start, you will have three basic mashing methods to choose from, and some equipment to select.

Regardless of your mashing method, you will need a four or five gallon kettle to use as a "mash tun." As the name suggests, this is the container where the mash is steeped. You will also need a second kettle of eight to ten gallons, in which to heat and hold your sparge water. In a commercial brewery, this tank would be called the "hot liquor collector." Probably, your boiling kettle, depending on its size, may be used as one of these containers. You will need, in any case, a boiling kettle capable of containing at least six gallons of boiling wort if you are making a five gallon batch.

The third piece of equipment is the "lauter tun" (see p. 42). After the mash, this is where the "goodies" are rinsed (sparged) out of the grains and collected in the boiling kettle. When you have to get as much extract as possible from the grain, a more elaborate setup is required than when you have only a limited amount of grain for color and flavor to supplement malt extracts. A number of systems are in use. This is the simplest and best for the kind of small scale brewing we do. You will need a five to seven gallon plastic bucket with a tight fitting lid, a plastic spigot with approximately a half inch opening, a large nylon straining bag which fits into the bucket, and a colander. Drill a hole in the side of the bucket about a half inch above the bottom, and attach the spigot. Cut a large hole in the center of the lid so that the colander can be fitted into it snugly. Push down the lid over the edges of the straining bag, holding it in position inside the bucket. That's the basic setup. When you're ready to sparge, scoop the mash into the straining bag inside the bucket, making sure the spigot is closed. Open the spigot and collect a quart or two of runoff. Pour it gently on top of the mash. Open the tap again and allow the mash to drain into a kettle. Put the colander in place, and begin scooping your sparge water into it, allowing the colander to spray it over the mash. Continue adding water until the water level rises to an inch or two above the grain. Drain the mash again. Continue filling and draining until the sparge water is used up or until the desired volume has been collected (6 gallons for a 5 gallon batch. This sparging system will work well no matter what mashing system has been employed.

The three mashing methods you'll have to choose from are, in order of complexity, Infusion, Upward Infusion, and Decoction.

Infusion mashing was traditionally employed with British malts, which are relatively low in both protein and enzyme content. This system uses a single temperature for starch conversion. Measure out 2¾ gallons of water for every 10 lbs. of grain, and heat it in your mash tun to a temperature approximately 10 degrees F. (6 C.) higher than the temperature you desire for your mash. In most cases, you will mash in somewhere between 150 and 158 degrees F. (66 and 70 C.), with the water, consequently, in the 160 to 170 degree range. Stir the cracked grain into the water. As you are in the range for converting starch to fermentable sugars, this temperature range is called a "sugar rest." You may begin to test for full starch conversion in approximately 30 minutes, though you can allow the mash to go on for as much as another hour if additional color or flavor components are desired. Then raise the temperature of the mash to 165 degrees F. 74 C.), timing it so the sparge water reaches the same temperature at about the same time. Then procede with your sparge as described earlier.

Upward Infusion is similar to standard infusion, except that the mash water is heated to only 130 degrees F. (54 C.) prior to mashing in. Thus, the initial mash temperature is approximately 120 degrees F. (49 C.). It is held there for 30 minutes, in what has traditionally been called a "protein rest." The temperaure is then raised to the "sugar rest" level. From that point, procede as with infusion. One of the keys here is that the enzymes which produce complete conversion to fermentable sugar are at their most active in the range between 130 and 135 degrees F. (54 to 57 C.), though the enzymes which produce dextrins instead, are most active between 150 and 158 degrees F. (66 and 70 C.). Thus, the time it takes you to pass from protein to sugar rest temperatures will, along with the sugar rest temperature selected, have a significant effect on the "full mouth feel," and the fermentability ratio of the beer, so you can make a number of different beers from the same ingredients.

Decoction is the third method. It comes from the European tradition, and is widely used in making lager beers. In this system, temperatures are raised by removing a portion of the mash, heating it to boiling, and then returning it to the rest of the mash. This can become rather involved, as there are single, double, and triple decoction systems, but just as an introduction, try a single decoction. Mash in at 120 degrees F. (49 C.) as with an upward infusion mash. After 30 minutes, remove about 40% of the mash (by volume), heat the removed portion to boiling, boil 20 minutes, and stir it back into the mash. This should bring you to the "sugar rest" temperature range. After a negative starch test raise the temperature and procede to sparge as with the other systems. Decoction gives you a slightly different caramelization of sugars than do the infusion systems, and therefore, a different flavor profile.

Whichever mashing system you choose, if you get this far with home brewing, you'll be well on your way to a lifetime of learning, enjoyment, and challenge. Here are a couple of recipes to begin with.

1. All Grain Light Lager—5 U.S. gal. (19 liters)

6 lbs. (2.7 kilos) Lager Malt
1 lb. (454 grams) Munich Malt
8 oz. (227 grams) Wheat Malt
2 oz. (57 grams) 100% Dextrin Powder
or 3 oz. (85 grams) Dextrine Malt
1 tsp. Gypsum
Bittering Hops to 24 bittering units
½ oz. (14 grams) Aromatic Hops
Water to five gallons (19 liters)
¾ cup Corn Sugar for priming
½ oz. (14 grams) Lager Yeast

Starting S.G.   45
Final S.G.   Will vary.

2. All Grain Pale Ale—5 U.S. gal. (19 liters)

7 lbs. (3.2 kilos) Pale Malt
1 lb. (454 grams) Munich Malt
8 oz. (227 grams) Crystal Malt
1½ tsp. Gypsum
1 Tbl. Irish Moss
⅛ tsp. Epsom Salts
½ tsp. Salt
Bittering Hops to 30 bittering units
½ oz. (14 grams) Aromatic Hops
Water to 5 gallons
¾ cup Corn Sugar for priming
½ oz. (14 grams) Ale Yeast

Starting S.G.   45
Final S.G.   Will vary.

Malt and Sugar Values

With one pound of the following ingredients per U.S. gallon of water, you may reasonably expect the following gravities. Grain yields, however, will be quite variable, depending on the efficiency of your grinding, mashing, and sparging systems.

Ingredient	Gravity
Malt Extract	36
Dry Malt	45
Corn Sugar	36
Cane Sugar	45
Brown Sugar	45
Rice Syrup	36
Dextrin Powder	45
Pale Malt	35
Lager Malt	35
Munich Malt	25
Mild Ale Malt	30
Crystal (Caramel) Malt	20
Wheat Malt	30
Dextrine Malt	28

Specific Gravity and Balling Equivalents

Balling	S.G.	Balling	S.G.
0	1.000	13	1.050
1	1.004	14	1.054
2	1.008	15	1.058
3	1.012	16	1.062
4	1.016	17	1.066
5	1.019	18	1.070
6	1.023	19	1.074
7	1.027	20	1.078
8	1.031	21	1.081
9	1.035	22	1.085
10	1.039	23	1.089
11	1.043	24	1.093
12	1.047		

Saccharometer Temperature Correction

Most saccharometers you will encounter are set to read correctly at 60 degrees F. (16 C.). If your sample is not at that temperature, you should correct your observed reading by adding or subtracting gravity points as indicated below.

Degrees C.	Degrees F.	Correction
0	32	Subtract 1.6
5	41	Subtract 1.3
10	50	Subtract .8
16	60	Read as observed.
20	68	Add 1.0
25	77	Add 2.2
30	86	Add 3.5
35	95	Add 5.0
40	104	Add 6.8
45	113	Add 8.8
50	122	Add 11.0
55	131	Add 13.3
60	140	Add 15.9

Note that these adjustments are for samples with a specific gravity of 40 (1.040). If your gravity is significantly lower, the corrections needed would be very slightly smaller. If it is significantly higher, the corrections would be slightly larger. It's unlikely, though, that home brewers will ever have to be quite that fine.

Fahrenheit and Celsius

To convert a Fahrenheit reading to Celsius, subtract 32 from the Fahrenheit figure, and divide the result by 1.8.

To convert a Celsius reading to Fahrenheit, multiply the Celsius figure by 1.8, and add 32 to the result.

Weight and Measure Equivalents

Fluid Measure

1 imperial gallon = 1.2 U.S. gallons (4.5459 liters)
1 U.S. gallon = .833 imperial gallon (3.7853 liters)
1 imperial fl. oz. = .961 U.S. fl. oz.
1 U.S. fl. oz. = 1.041 imperial fl. oz.
1 imperial pint = 20 imperial fl. oz.
1 U.S. cup = 8 U.S. fl. oz. (.5 U.S. pint, .417 imperial pint)

Weight Measure

There is no difference between U.S. and imperial weights.

1 oz. = 28.35 grams
1 lb. (16 oz.) = 453.592 grams (.45359 kilograms)
1 kilogram (1,000 grams) = 35.274 oz. (2.2046 lbs.)

ANNOTATED BIBLIOGRAPHY

Anderson, Stanley, with Hull, Raymond. *The Art of Making Beer.*
New York: Hawthorne Books, Inc. 1971.

This is one of the first "modern" home brewing books published in North America. Anderson, president of a chain of winemaking and brewing supply shops headquartered in Canada, made a considerable contribution in the early 1970s. The book was marred only by a tendency to list items by the brand names of his company. Unless a new edition is forthcoming, however, it has become a bit dated, though there's still some good workable information here.

Berry, C.J.J. *Home Brewed Beers and Stouts.* 5th ed. Andover, England: The Amateur Winemaker, 1981.

Home Brewed Beers and Stouts, first published in 1963, is probably the ancestor of us all. I consider it the first modern home brewing text. It helped launch the movement in Britain, which, in turn, launched us. It contains, of course, a number of recipes which are still good today.

Broderick, Harold M. (ed.). *The Practical Brewer.* Madison, Wisconsin: The Master Brewers Association of the Americas, 1977.

If you're a serious brewer going on to the commercial literature, here is where you start. This book is a manual for people going to work at commercial breweries, and is a gold mine of information.

Eckhardt, Fred. *A Treatise on Lager Beers.* 7th ed. Portland, Oregon: Hobby Winemaker, 1983.

I have a special fondness for this book, because I began making beer, using it as a guide, shortly after the first edition was published, back in 1970. It specializes in lagers, and requires intense scrutiny, because there are a lot of nuggets tucked away in odd corners throughout the text. This book belongs in every home brewer's library.

Hough, J.S., Briggs, D.E., Stevens, R., and Young, T.W. *Malting and Brewing Science.* 2nd ed. London and New York: Chapman and Hall, 1981, 1982.

Without doubt, *Malting and Brewing Science* is the "Bible" of the brewing industry at the present time. It is, however, only for those who wish to venture deeply into the commercial brewing literature.

Jackson, Michael. *The World Guide to Beer.* Englewood Cliffs, New Jersey: Prentice-Hall, Inc., 1971.

This is not, of course, a book on brewing, but is instead, a glorious celebration of beer. It merits inclusion here, not only because it is of major interest to all lovers of beer, but because there is considerable information that will help you refine your awareness and understanding of beer styles. That, in turn, will benefit your brewing.

Line, Dave. *Brewing Beers Like Those You Buy.* Andover, England: The Amateur Winemaker, 1978.

If you're looking for a collection of recipes designed to duplicate many of the world's beers, this book is a must.

Line, Dave. *The Big Book of Brewing.* Andover, England: The Amateur Winemaker, 1974.

This is the classic work focusing on grain brewing in England. If you are heading toward advanced brewing, you will want to make a lengthy stop here. As you might expect, the emphasis is on ales and stouts.

Mares, William. *Making Beer.* New York: Alfred A Knopf, Inc., 1984.

In brewing, as in life, it's sometimes necessary to stop and do something just for the sheer enjoyment of it. Reading this book (by a Vermont humorist and home brewer) comes under this dictum. It is a homebrewer's odyssey through the hobby, filled with sagacity and good fun. The last part of this book is required reading for any home brewer dreaming about starting a commercial brewery.

Miller, David. *Home Brewing for Americans.* Andover, England: The Amateur Winemaker, 1981.

The first author to write specifically for America's advanced home brewers, Miller provides a great deal of information useful for all-grain brewers. He helps you understand the "whys" of some of the "whats."

Noonan, Gregory J. *Brewing Lager Beer*. Boulder, Colorado: Brewers Publications (a division of American Homebrewers Association), 1986.

This new book is the first comprehensive work for advanced home brewers and small commercial brewers with an emphasis on lager beers. The gap between the homebrewing and commercial literatures is expertly bridged, providing much needed support for anyone attempting to make the transition. Impressive as Noonan's technical grasp is, his ability to render difficult topics comprehensible is even more so. Many brewers will find the chapter on water to be worth the book's price by itself, though there is much more here than that. This book should become a classic. If you have any aspirations toward advanced brewing you should own a copy.

Papazian, Charlie. *The New and Complete Joy of Home Brewing*. New York: Avon Books, 1984.

Though I don't really believe a single book will ever be "complete" in the sense of definitive, this book is otherwise aptly named. No one comes to brewing more joyfully, or more ambitiously than Papazian. This is a large book, packed with information and insight. It could use a better fermentation method for beginners, and an index. Every home brewer, however, should have this one.

Pollock, J.R.A. (ed.). *Brewing Science*. New York: Academic Press, 1979, 1981.

This is a weighty, commercial text for only the most serious. The information, however, is excellent.

In addition to these books, there are three more sources worthy of mention, a video and two periodicals.

Conner, Jay. *The Way to Make Beer*. Novato, California: Paperback Video, 1985.

For the first time it is possible to learn home brewing from a video. In this one hour presentation, Conner takes beginning brewers through the basics with a common sense approach. It is always helpful for prospective brewers to see the process before they start. It is also a good way to learn home brewing if one's reading skills are limited.

Eckhardt, Fred, and Owens, Bill (eds.). *Amateur Brewer Communications*. Hayward, California: Amateur Brewer Information Service, all issues.

For some years, Eckhardt has put out occasional publications on the general subjects of beer and brewing. The titles have varied, and the schedule has been erratic as well, but the publications have always been enjoyed, and many articles have been excellent. As this is written, Owens, owner of Buffalo Bill's, a California brewpub, has just joined the team. As nothing has yet emerged since the reorganization, the future is hard to predict. One hopes for the same solid information coming out a bit more regularly than in the past.

Papazian, Charlie (ed.). *Zymurgy*. Boulder, Colorado: The American Homebrewers Association, all issues.

The temptation to call *Zymurgy* magazine "the last word in home brewing periodicals" is, unfortunately, irresistible. Nonetheless, the designation is accurate in every sense. The journal of the American Homebrewers Association, it has become an absolutely first class magazine, eagerly awaited by home brewers around the world. Published quarterly, with one additional special issue per year, it contains information to interest the most serious brewer, but keeps things in perspective with relaxed good humor. If you want to get more out of home brewing, subscribe to *Zymurgy*.

INDEX

ABOUT THE AUTHOR

Mr. Burch is internationally recognized as an expert in home brewing and winemaking, and has been instructing others in these arts since 1972. He has been co-owner of Great Fermentations, a home brew supply company with outlets in San Rafael and Santa Rosa, California, since its founding in 1978. His first book, *Quality Brewing,* was a major influence on the growing home brew movement during the 1970s and early 1980s. He has addressed both the American Homebrewers Association's and the Home Wine and Beer Trade Association's national conferences, and been a frequent contributor to the AHA's quarterly journal, *Zymurgy.* In 1986 he earned the title "Homebrewer of the Year" by sweeping best of show honors at the AHA's annual competition, winning against entries from 40 states and several Canadian provinces.

THE AMERICAN HOMEBREWERS ASSOCIATION

Join the Thousands of Homebrewers Who Read Zymurgy

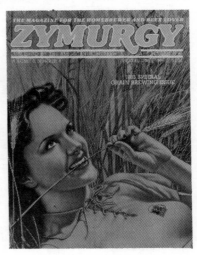

Zymurgy—A Magazine for Homebrewers and Beer Lovers

Learn What's New in Homebrewing Including:

New Recipes • Product Reviews • Tips for Beginners • New Brewing Techniques • Equipment and Ingredients • Beer News • Beer History • And Much, Much More!

SATISFACTION GUARANTEED!

Published five times a year by the American Homebrewers Association

Mail This Coupon Today!

_____ ENCLOSED IS $17 FOR ONE FULL YEAR.
    (CANADIAN/FOREIGN SUBSCRIPTIONS ARE $22 U.S.)
_____ PLEASE CHARGE MY CREDIT CARD
OR CALL NOW FOR CREDIT CARD ORDER AT 303- 447-0816

VISA _____ MC _____ CARD NO. _____
EXP. DATE _____ SIGNATURE _____
NAME _____
ADDRESS _____
CITY _____ STATE _____ ZIP _____

Make Check to: Zymurgy, P.O.Box 287-Q, Boulder, CO 80306

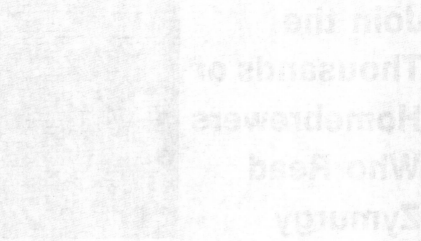